FIRST AID FOR HEROES

Written by
Jane H. Davis

CREDITS

Written by Jane H. Davis
Cover Illustration by Ann F. Cummings

Edited by   Frank Monahan
Art Direction   Meredith Hancock

Published by Rocket Science Productions

© Copyright August 2011 Jane H. Davis

ISBN-13   978-1-937121-06-8

Library of Congress Control Number   2011935669

INTRODUCTION

We are fast approaching the ten year anniversary of 9/11/01. As I sit at my computer pondering my final chapter, I look back on these past ten years, and wonder, what would I change? Periodically, I want to change it all…the agglomeration of negativity, hatred, pain and illness that exists in our world. At times I want to have the collective ten years be eradicated from the face of the earth.

We all wish 9/11 hadn't happened, don't we? It is astonishing that this single day in our nation's history could create such a dramatic chain of events, drastically affecting and altering so many lives, and it continues. It was one of the many defining moments our nation has had to endure. Positively, our country rallied for a common cause; we became extremely proud Americans, waving our flags, donating, volunteering, and protecting. We continue to read in the papers of those who sacrificed their lives to work on the Pile at Ground Zero, succumbing to the many health issue associated from their selfless toils those days, weeks and months after. Such true heroes they were and still are! We have lost and continue to lose too many of our proud upstanding Americans in the military to the war on terrorism. Our heroes' sacrifices for our country will never be forgotten.

Everyone remembers where they were and what they were doing on that tragic day. Each person has their own story. This book is about my story, the days leading up to 9/11 and then my experiences after, the past ten years.

Life is tenuous and we challenge ourselves to keep it

in some sort of balance. When there is a negative, there is a positive. Embracing these challenges is what I find makes life rewarding. I have dealt with an enormous amount over these past ten years and what I have learned has been immeasurable. The challenges I have faced during many uncertain times and the roles I have taken will continue to prepare me to become the strongest individual I can be. Where would we be without challenges? You know, life is always going to throw you a curve ball; it is up to you on how you catch it.

This book would not be in existence if it wasn't for Alison Dubois. She believed in me and believed in my story. Two and a half years ago, I signed up for an online writing class on *How to Write your Memoirs*, Alison was my instructor. After completing the assignments and passing the course, Alison emailed me and asked, "Jane what are you going to do with your story?" With minimal encouragement she suggested I write a book. Without her support and guidance I would not be where I am today. Thank you Alison for believing in me!

Yes there are many positive features in my life to include my husband, Gary, my two children, their spouses, and my three, almost four, grandchildren! Thank you to my family and countless friends who stood by me and supported me throughout this process. You have all been my cheerleaders! Ann Cummings, my niece in-law, was the awesome artist for my cover. You are amazing!

I need to give a very special thank you to my husband Gary. We have been through it, haven't we? And we have survived those ups and downs, highs and lows. Thank you for your support, appreciation and love that you have given to me. No more curve balls, okay?

CHAPTER 1

What's *That* Smell?

"I can't smell that *smell* anymore!" I exclaimed to my sister Melissa as I stood overseeing the area that was nothing like it had been eight years earlier. I had returned, with my family, for a visit to the hallowed grounds of what used to be the World Trade Center about a year ago. Standing there, I felt both estranged and like the biblical story of the wayward prodigal son that had returned home.

So much had changed since that dreadful day. Besides the obvious cleanup, which helped and was necessary, New Yorkers had rebuilt some of its buildings and repaired others. Seeing the positive changes made me feel hopeful as well.

"What do you mean Janie?" Melissa asked bringing my focus back to Ground Zero.

This was my sister's first visit to the Ground Zero site. Since she'd come to do the tour with me, I took my time trying to explain it to her. I wanted her to understand and I wanted her to feel the emotion, or at least a sense of what I felt. What I felt was that it was extremely important to me to share this with her.

Melissa had become such a close sister and friend to me over the years. We didn't start with such closeness as children, but as we grew into adulthood and shared so many experiences, the bond had been formed. Now she was here to share one of my experiences, one I hope she could understand.

"The terrible smell is finally not here, though I assume in reality that it has been gone for a long time," I said. "Odd that I smelled it last year, it must have been all in my mind," I said softly, more to myself than to her. It had been almost eight years since that tragic event, but it still felt fresh to me.

2

The overwhelming feelings came flooding back as I began to remember events that I had forgotten or perhaps couldn't bear to recall during that chaotic time. It's funny how the human brain will work to shield us from our own ugliness. But I was thankful, because at the time, I couldn't have handled any more than I did.

I have been back to Ground Zero about five times since my days of volunteering after 9/11. Each time I return, more memories work their way to the top, like bubbles in water floating and finding their way to the surface. And each time those memories return, so does another wave of pain. Our country and its people were just raw and many still are experiencing that rawness.

Gary, my husband, and I, along with my sister and her husband, Mark, had come to New York City for the weekend in August 2009. Each time Gary comes back with me to the site, he learns a little more about the six and a half weeks I spent working as a Red Cross volunteer nurse right on the edge of the Ground Zero site.

"Here is the bridge that was standing", I pointed it out to them, as if I were some tour guide. "See this white bridge?" I continued. "Just below it is where I brought the ill rescue workers that often needed more first aid care than I could give them. There was a group of doctors, the DMAT (Disaster Medical Assistant Team), whose job was to take care of the more critically ill and injured. I would either walk, or get a ride on a golf cart from my Respite Center, across the 'pile' and then back to the to the respite area," I explained.

"It was a long walk", I reminisced. "I would see those firefighters and rescue workers climbing on the pile in the dark with the flood lights lighting up the site, the pile, as if it were day time. There were always the rescuers watching

3

those individuals working on the pile. They never would turn their backs on their comrades; they would just watch and watch. Sometimes when I walked back from the DMAT they would turn and talk to me and thank me for being there and helping. Can you believe it, they thanked *me*? They were working so hard trying to find human remains but they thanked me? It still blows my mind." I felt the lump in my throat growing. *Swallow, Jane, hold it together. Show your sister you are strong!*

As I talk, more memories push to the surface. I can see in my mind the lingering smoke around the Ground Zero area and smell the stench of debris, some of it coming from charred flesh. I shiver shaking off the memory and hear my sister's voice.

"So where was *your* building?" she asks.

"On the other side of the site at St. John's University, just one block past the site, on Murray Street" I said pointing toward the university. "The American Red Cross took over the building and used it as a Respite Center for those that were working at the Ground Zero site. It was a place that they could go and just relax, eat, get first aid, talk, watch television, play on the computer, well it had just about everything one could imagine! It even had a place in it where the rescue workers could get massages!"

"The first place I volunteered at was at a Public School located at West St. just about a block from where I got off the subway. I asked my supervisor that first day, *how do I know where my building is?* She said: Yours is the one with the huge American flag covering the entire front of the building. It was impossible to miss."

It was a thrill to me, they were finally rebuilding! It made me feel hopeful. I was glad. I believed the American public needed that. It was a very slow process but I could see that

4

there was some progression since I had been there the year before.

Americans still considered it a scar in the middle of lower Manhattan. There will always be that scar in my mind and in the minds of millions of others, but knowing that they are rebuilding is a great relief to me. Each time I go and see more construction being done, it becomes very cathartic for me as if each beam being put in place is somehow helping me heal.

Two construction workers see me looking through the fence at the site and come by to chat with me. One guy was tall and fair, the other man was shorter and dark. I guess they could tell by the look on my face that I was struggling a bit with my emotions.

"You okay lady?" the taller guy asked.

"Yes", I assured them. "I used to be a volunteer here right after the attacks," I explained. They nodded.

"God bless you for helping," the shorter guy said. I smiled and nodded.

I told them that it was so good to see the building being redone. I thanked them for making it happen and shook their hands. *I am growing, I am healing,* I thought, *I did this without so many tears this time.* But next time, who knows, the tears may fall freely.

"St. Paul's Church is right here," I said, returning the focus to my little group. "It is still standing because the north WTC tower fell in a different direction." As if by divine intervention, the north tower fell to the west and slightly north of the church. Though it was carpeted in dust and debris, it escaped serious damage. "The church became a center for rescue workers as well as a shrine where desperate relatives would leave flyers with photos of the missing", I reminisced as I spoke to them. "There would be flowers, candles, poems and other gifts left behind." I continued. In a weird way, I felt strange to be describing the event like some celebrity highlights. Only these highlights were not celebrity tidbits, it was a blemish on America that permanently marred us.

We then walked the path that I took to my apartment in Battery Park City where I stayed while I was volunteering. I took a deep breath.

"Every day," I told them, "as I finished work and headed to my apartment I would have to walk by the Teddy Bear Wall." It was also an area where family and friends could leave memorabilia of their loved ones. It is now devoid of these artifacts and just stands as a naked wall. I took a picture of it. "It was so very painful for me to walk by that on a daily basis," I said feeling that old sadness returning. "Most days, I would shield my eyes so as not to see this wall. I was living and breathing Ground Zero daily and I needed some down time to clear my mind."

"Here's the spot where Rudy Giuliani shook my hand, along with the President of the Philippines, Gloria Macapagal-Arroyo!" I exclaimed. Gary, my husband, had come to visit me in November of 2001, and he and I were taking a tour of the outside perimeter of the WTC site when Mayor Giuliani approached. "They both walked directly over to us and thanked me for all I was doing to help at the site." I guess I was pretty obvious as I was wearing my Red Cross vest and hardhat at the time, so I was visible as part of the team.

Suddenly, another memory came flooding back to me, as it always does every time I come to Manhattan. Unlike the many memorable moments, this one wasn't pleasant. Would my stalker be out here looking for me? Would he know where I was? I decided not to mention it this time when

I came into the city; it was my own private concern. But someday I hope to be able to come to the area and not always be looking over my shoulder, wondering if *he* is still out there. Would I always be afraid that one day he'll suddenly show up?

"I am so in awe of what you did Janie. Thank you so much for sharing this difficult time in your life with us, it means so much to me to get this tour from you. I can sense that it still is very painful for you to be here and to talk about, but thank you. This has impacted my life!" Melissa reached for me and hugged me so tight then tenderly kissed my cheek.

Daily I am forced to remember my six and a half weeks here because of the cough I've inherited that makes me need to use an inhaler. Sometimes I have a lot of difficulty catching my breath, all this as a backlash for my time at Ground Zero. Other days I am so hoarse that I can hardly utter a simple sentence. I'm not alone of course, so many of us (volunteers) that were in this area are suffering from these and many more side effects today.

But on the bright side, I have always been drawn to the wonderful city of New York. Thank goodness, Gary is too! Several years ago, we even bought a time-share near Central Park so that we could visit this wonderful city at least twice a year. We have since visited the Ground Zero site almost every time we come to town. Some visits to the area are more difficult than others, but as time goes by, I know that I am slowly beginning to heal. But no matter how much time passes, the memories will never leave me, ever.

CHAPTER 2

Business as Usual
Five days remaining...

The alarm sounded. Green numbers shone, it was 6:30 a.m. My sleepy fingers randomly began pressing buttons, hoping to find the correct one, waiting for my eyes to focus. I rolled back over as I wasn't feeling particularly motivated to get up but I knew my running buddies would eagerly be waiting for me down the block in less than thirty minutes just as they were every Thursday morning. Oh my God, thirty minutes, what was I doing? I *needed* to scramble.

I am an Army spouse and I live with my husband Gary at Ft. Bragg, North Carolina which is his latest post assignment. He is commanding the hospital, Womack Army Medical Center. I am also a Registered Nurse and a volunteer for the American Red Cross at Fort Bragg holding the title of advisor. I sit on many committees throughout Fort Bragg that include some advisory roles. It is what happens to so many of us when our spouses hold senior positions in the military.

With my duties as an Army wife, I can often find myself feeling overwhelmed. Today was no exception. There were committees and meetings for just about everything, some that I chair or am the president, but all of which I am expected to run in a cohesive and organized fashion! It can be trying to be an Army spouse sometimes. I wouldn't trade it for the world, but it just seems so intense when I am right in the middle of it.

I started running to alleviate some of the tension and to be doing something that was just *mine*. But even running sometimes loses its appeal. I like the exercise (and need it, to be honest) and visiting with the other officer's spouses helps, but the schedule I am expected to keep at times is absolutely grueling.

None-the-less by 6:50 a.m., I was out the door grumbling under my breath but jogging towards my friends just the same. Within moments I spied two of my pals huddled together, running in place, anxiously waiting. Both waved, I waved back.

"Good morning," I said to Barb and Debbie.

Debbie is tall, blonde and ambitious. She runs out of vanity. She and I are not really close but we manage to maintain a decent rapport for appearances. Barb on the other hand, is short and dark, just barely five feet. She struggles with her weight and needs to run to stay in shape.

Right away I formed an alliance with Barb and before long our respective husbands became good friends. Barb is the kind of person that I always hoped I'd connect with each time my husband had to be re-stationed. Being an army spouse sometimes has its drawbacks, and that was one of them, never knowing what we would be walking into at each new place.

Even though Barb had become a good friend, it has been a friendship that I have had to work hard to cultivate. I know Barb likes me and it definitely helps that our husbands are both Army guys, but still the woman can be quite opinionated and aloof at times. I know to take baby steps with her, not to push our friendship.

It was one more reason why I felt like I had been lucky over the years to make those few special friends special while also seeing, visiting and living in parts of the country that I wouldn't ordinarily visit. It makes me thankful for this kind of family I have acquired.

"Where are you?" Barb asked, noticing my distraction.

"Oh nothing," I assured her. "I was just thinking that I get to see my grandson tomorrow and I'm really looking forward to it," I told her bubbling with enthusiasm. Barb smiled in a

11

knowing way.

"It's like that for me too when Phil brings over his kids. Sometimes you just need that change of pace."

"Yes, you do. And I've got three more meetings, one this morning and two this afternoon to get through," I confided just as two more women came in line to join the group. "Of which I don't really have any interest in," I added. They jogged towards us, the shorter one with longer hair was Lois and her taller companion was Nancy.

"Are we ready?" Debbie asked everyone. There was a general consensus of groans and lackluster agreement. "Then let's go ladies, I guess I can say ladies as Dave can't join us today." Debbie encouraged as she sprinted ahead occasionally glancing back.

"We're all going to get there at the same time," Barb chided.

"Don't tell her that," I told her chuckling.

"Absolutely no way!" Barb said.

The sun was bright and high in the sky. I knew what that meant, it was going to be another warm one. Fort Bragg had been locked in a heat wave for nearly a week. The heat each night had left us feeling tired and depleted.

For nearly an hour the five of us continued jogging along the familiar terrain of Fort Bragg's neighborhoods as we intermittently shared idle chit chat. Then Debbie corralled the group back in front of the statue of Iron Mike which was where we always start and conclude our runs. The group had chosen the statue as a meeting place because it was centrally located for each of the runners which made it convenient. Because of this wonderful statue, we named our group, *The Iron Mike Runners*. Iron Mike was the common nickname for the Airborne Trooper Statue built in 1960-61 to commemorate America's WWII fighting men.

Almost right away Lois and Nancy excused themselves saying they needed to "make breakfast" for their families. Debbie stalled watching Barb and me.

"Does anyone want a cup of coffee?" she offered.

"I have to pass Deb, I need to get back and get ready to meet with the medical wives for the upcoming Welcome Coffee on the 11th," I told her.

"Barb?" Debbie pressed.

"Rain check," Barb said.

Deb shrugged then started jogging towards her own place. She waved at us over her shoulder.

"Bye," Barb and I said in unison. Then she asked: "Do you really have to go?"

"Yes I do. I'm sorry. Next time," I assured her taking Barb's hand for a moment. She nodded.

"Enjoy that grandson of yours," she said then veered off.

"I will," I told her while looking at my watch. "Where does the time go? I better hurry," I mumbled to myself.

CHAPTER 3

The Calm Before the Storm

I was excited to be seeing my one and only grandson, JT. Often seeing him was my only reprieve from a much cluttered Army (spouse) routine. I loved my husband Gary and our life but there were times when I was a bit envious of friends who did not have an endless sea of meetings and groups. The expectations for each were taking a toll. Sometimes spending time with my grandson and just enjoying the mundane was exactly what I needed.

As usual, I was meeting my daughter Elizabeth at the Burger King in Lillington, NC. We picked the Burger King in Lillington as it was midway between where Elizabeth and I lived. It took me about twenty minutes to get there from my house, but getting a chance to visit with JT was worth it.

As I pulled the car into the Burger King parking lot I could already see Elizabeth and JT standing just outside the entrance. Quickly I parked and began heading their way.

Almost immediately Elizabeth saw me and pointed at me to JT.

"Look JT, there's Umma," she told him. That was the name, Umma, that JT decided to call me and I loved it! Right away the small boy, that was no more than a toddler identified his grandma and begin to excitedly squirm.

"Umma, Umma!" he called as he ran to me when I was only a few feet from them. Right away I scooped him up and gave him a big hug.

"How's my big guy?" I asked him.

"Hi Umma! Mommy got me a hot wheels car, wanna see?" JT produced a black plastic car toy with flames painted on the sides of the toy.

"Oh, that's a real beauty", I told him.

JT agreed as his attention stayed focused on the car toy

throughout their visit, which allowed me and Elizabeth to talk freely. I could tell that my daughter was in an especially somber mood.

"How's it going?" I asked my daughter.

"Well, James' hours are being cut. I still have twelve more hours of education to get in before I can get a job, so things are a little tight," Elizabeth confessed looking a bit bashful. I was shocked. Obviously my daughter had not wanted me to know, as she had kept the information pretty guarded. I tried not to show my obvious concern.

"Oh honey, why didn't you tell me? Do you need help? You know that dad and I will be glad to help you" I offered. Elizabeth looked at me. It was clear from the look on her face that this was not a subject she liked to discuss, especially with her mother. Elizabeth shook her head.

"No, we're all right, but thanks!" Elizabeth said a little too quickly.

"Honey…" I started. Elizabeth brought her hand up. I became quiet.

"I didn't tell you that because I was looking for a hand out. You asked me how I was doing, so I told you. Now can we drop this?" she asked. I knew my daughter's gestures well and this one was her way of dismissing the subject. *Back off Jane*, I thought, *now is not the time to nag. When the time is ready, she will talk, she always does.*

"So what have you two been up to lately?" I asked, trying to shift the conversation to a more benign topic and hopefully improve the atmosphere.

"We took JT to the movies last weekend," Elizabeth volunteered. I smiled. I saw so much of myself in Elizabeth, that familiar willingness and need to please her mother.

A sobering thought crossed my mind, my relationship

with my own mother. It had never been optimum, but over time we had at least managed to be civil to each other.
The starkness of that reality made me concerned. Why did Elizabeth feel such a need? Was I more like my mother than I dared to think?

"Mom," Elizabeth nudged me. I focused and suddenly realized that I was holding up the ordering line at the window. I blushed.

"Sorry," I said to the people behind them and quickly stepped up to the counter.

As we ate our lunch I was torn between watching JT and Elizabeth. I loved my daughter so much, wanted everything for her. I wanted our relationship to be so different from my own difficulties with my mother. Elizabeth noticed my quiescence.

"Are you okay?"she asked.

"I'm great." I told her. Elizabeth looked skeptical.

"Are you ready to go with Umma?" Elizabeth asked JT. The boy squirmed excitedly in his seat.

"Umma!" he sputtered. I smiled at him, looking at that sweet angelic face of his.

We walked out to Elizabeth's car. Liz handed me a tote bag for JT, filled with a few toys, several changes of clothes and pajamas.

"It has all of his "stuff" in there!" Elizabeth chuckled.

"It'll be fine." I said wrestling with the heavy tote. "I'll bring him back on Monday, though by the feel of this, it looks like he is staying for a month!"

"Ha ha" Elizabeth laughed "I just never know how much to pack. He's going to love, hanging with you guys," Elizabeth told me as we exchanged hugs.

"I love you," I told her. "Enjoy some quiet time okay?"

"I love you too. Now stop worrying!" My daughter chastised, waving me off.

I then took JT's hand and began towards car.

"Umma tar!" he exclaimed. That was his name for my little green VW bug.

"You ready to see Fwah?" I asked him. The toddler's eyes lit up. "Fwah!" he squealed.

Fwah was the name JT gave to Gary, his version of Granddaddy. I laughed when he said it, reminiscing about the day that he decided to call Gary that name. It was the summer of 2000 and we were getting ready to depart Fort Rucker, Alabama. Elizabeth and JT came to watch Gary's Change of Command as outgoing commander of the hospital. We were all sitting outside in our carport and Elizabeth asked Gary what he wanted JT to call him.

"Sir" he joked. We all laughed and said "NO WAY!"

"How about Colonel?" Gary said teasing.

"Try again" I said

"Okay, he can call me Granddaddy" he acquiesced. With that JT looked at him and then at all of us and got a devilish smile on his face and said "Fwahdaddy"

Hence the name, shortened to Fwah. This name is now used by my children, their spouses and all of my grandchildren and even sometimes by me!

"I guess that's a 'yes'," I said as I belted JT in his car seat and watched Elizabeth's car exiting the parking lot. "Okay, it's me and you kiddo", I said closing the car door.

CHAPTER 4

Impact!
Hours remaining: 0
Date 9/11/01

I rounded the corner of Randolph Street before starting to sprint into Ft. Bragg's row of houses for their officers and military service men and women. I was on my way to Missy's to discuss the final Medical Wives coffee meeting preparation we had planned for that evening. But before I could get to her house, I was immediately met by Missy running towards me frantically.

"Jane! Jane! Have you heard?" She came bounding up to me very animated. I stopped, and then half bent still struggling to catch my breath.

"Heard what?" I asked.

It was clear that Missy was greatly disturbed but by what I did not know yet. But I saw the vivid fear in Missy's eyes and wondered what could be so wrong as to make her react this way. All the same, the sudden show of emotion was surprising to me.

"The to—ooowers, Twin Towers!" Missy sputtered desperately trying to enunciate the words she could barely utter. She was very animated as she directed me to come with her. Reluctantly I followed.

Once inside Missy immediately began pointing to the small television set she had resting on her kitchen counter. A breaking news ribbon was running across the bottom of the screen as my eyes watched a plane descend head on into the south tower. "Oh my God," the words were in my throat but I couldn't get them out.

I looked at Missy, the shock transparent on her face. My

first impulse was to disbelieve what my own eyes had just witnessed.

"I think they're replaying what I just saw," Missy told me whose eyes were the size of saucers. My brain was still fuzzy. I didn't want to believe it; it was just too hard to comprehend. What did this mean to our country, to our national security?

"Missy…" I said slowly. Just as the news commentator came on informing viewers that both towers had been hit. "Oh my God, we just watched the plane hit the building!" My hands automatically went to my mouth.

"Did he say 'both'?" Missy asked incredulous. I just nodded, unable to respond.

In my mind thoughts of panic and disbelief overlapped. I felt half-frozen, unsure of how to respond. My only concrete reasoning was that I did not want to be in Missy's house, I needed to get home to *my house, my family*.

Equally my mind began assaulting me with worries about my kids, if they were okay, if my grandson, JT that I'd held so dear and had seen in less than 24 hours earlier was okay. I had to know that no matter what else was going on in the world or would happen that my family was okay. The possibility that harm could touch them made me paralyzed. I needed to get home. *Now.*

"I'm s-sorry Missy. I have to go," I said taking her hand. "I have to be with my family now."

Missy looked a little shell-shocked. Suddenly she squeezed my hand back and nodded.

"I understand," she said softly. For a moment, I hesitated, seeing Missy so vulnerable had caught me off guard. The normal scatter-brained demeanor she'd become accustomed to had been replaced by a frightened young woman.

"You have my number Missy, call me later, and let me know that you and Joe are okay?" I added while heading for the door. I left with Missy still standing in the middle of her kitchen.

Such a picture of my neighbor and fellow Army wife made me concerned, and yet I felt strongly that my first duties were towards my own family. I needed to know that Gary and my kids and my precious grandson JT, were all okay.

Even though my house was less than five minutes away, somehow that morning I made it there in a matter of seconds, or so it seemed. I was so anxious to see Gary's face that I left the front door wide open as I began checking every room.

No Gary. Then I noticed the time on the clock in the kitchen. It read 9:15. That meant Gary would be at work, at the hospital. A wave of panic swept over me. I had to know that he was okay. Even if I couldn't see his face, I still desperately needed to hear his voice.

I clutched the kitchen phone and dialed his office phone. Each time it rang, I could feel my heart doing a double flip.

"Come on", I heard myself say. "Answer!" But Gary didn't, instead his number just rang.

"Hello?" I heard Valerie's voice, Gary's secretary. A wave of relief swept over.

"Oh, Thank God. Val, where's Gary?" I asked trying not to panic.

"He's doing his hospital rounds. Are you okay?" Valerie asked.

For a moment, I fought the impulse to go to the hospital, then my mind clicked into rescue mode and I began to blurt out what I'd just seen and heard on the television, my worries, and my concern. I heard Valerie gasp as I revealed the details.

"Oh my God, Jane," she said. "I'll reach Colonel Matteson and tell him, actually I will tell everyone!" she promised.

"Thank you, Val and please have him call me when he gets a free minute," I said quickly followed by my goodbye, and then instinctively I dialed the Red Cross Station, located on Fort Bragg.

The phone rang busy. I dialed again. Busy. Over and over, I heard the menacing busy tone. Finally, I tried Kathy's cell phone. Kathy was the Station Manager, a working buddy.

"Hello?" Kathy said.

"Kathy, oh thank God. What is happening? The line was busy. Sorry to call you on your cell Kathy but I couldn't get through," I explained sheepishly.

"Jane, the towers were bombed. Of course you can't get through. Everyone is calling. Giuliani has already declared that New York is in a state of emergency. Please stop calling, we need to keep those lines open for emergency help." She told me emphatically.

A million thoughts were spinning through my mind. All of them had a familiar theme; first, I needed to know my family was okay followed by needing to do something to help. Ever since my college days, I had felt compelled to get involved in community projects. If there was a need, I was there. It had started as a child, helping the neighborhood causes, money for orphanages, always wanting to give money to those less fortunate. It was a powerful drive within me, compelling me, prompting to help, somehow. I had to.

"Let me help, Kathy", I persisted.

"We're not ready for that Jane, it's too soon. Nothing has been organized yet." She scolded.

"There must be something," I insisted.

"Jane, there isn't. You know you can trust me, I'd tell you, okay?"

"O-kay," I said reluctantly.

The phone beeped. I looked at the caller I.D.; it was my daughter. My heart skipped.

"Kathy, I gotta go, but please call me, tell me what I can do. I have to do something. Okay?" I pleaded.

"I will, Jane. As soon as I know something, you'll know something. Okay?"

"Great", I said, and then switched my phone over to catch Elizabeth.

"Elizabeth, oh thank God! How are you?" I could hear myself gushing with relief. At least *she* was okay.

"Mom, I'm fine but I can't believe this," she said. My eyes automatically welled with tears.

"I've been so worried." I admitted.

"Oh Mom, we're fine", Elizabeth assured. Elizabeth knew my nature to fret until I was sure everything was okay. "I just wanted to make sure you'd heard," Elizabeth told me.

"Missy pulled me into her house this morning, we saw the second plane hit the South Tower," I said. For a moment, the image replayed in my mind as another sweep of emotion brushed over. Then it hit me, our country was under attack.

Again, I felt pulled to help. I had volunteered before when there was a need. I was ready to do it again.

"Oh Mom, that's awful. Have you talked to Dad?"

"I haven't been able to get a hold of him," I confessed.

"You try him, I'll try Ian," she said. Ian is my son and was at school in Raleigh, North Carolina at NC State.

"Yes, talk to Ian. Then let me know." I instructed trying

to keep my wits about me and not to sound as fearful as I felt. "So, how's my favorite grandson?"

"Ha ha, he's your only grandson! He's fine, Mom, we both are. Now stop worrying, okay?" Elizabeth waited. I could feel myself taking a breath. I *knew* that tone, Elizabeth was worried too.

"Okay, call me later", I instructed. I heard Elizabeth promise as she set down the phone. I put the phone back in its cradle then grabbed my purse. If I couldn't reach him by phone, I was bound and determined that I'd track him down, somehow.

CHAPTER 5

Helpless

"Kathy, it's Jane again, please tell me what I can do to help", I pleaded into the phone hoping that Kathy, the Red Cross Station Manager would finally give me something to do. All morning I felt glued to the television, listening and watching every piece of news as it unfolded. I felt overwhelmed, antsy, pent up energy was coursing through my veins. I HAD to do something, anything! By now, both towers had crumbled and the television stations played the scene over and over.

"Oh, all right Jane; you might as well come in, at least having you here will open up the phone lines!" Kathy said with a heavy sigh.

"I'm sorry I've called so much, it's just I can't sit at home and watch this on the news any more! It is freaking me out! God, now it is the Pentagon too and then the plane crash in Pennsylvania. What the hell is going on?" I asked with dismay. "I've been in touch with all of my family and friends and all anyone can do is cry, I have to do more Kathy!"

"I'll see you in a few minutes, I've got to go, there are a million people calling us!" she exclaimed.

Why was it so important that I was in contact with my whole family? I just had to hear everyone's voices to know that they were okay. My mother was so nervous about the day's events and I had to keep re-assuring her that everything was very secure on the military post and that nothing was going to happen to Gary and me. I was so pleased to finally hear from my son Ian. North Carolina State classes had been canceled for the day. He had been online on his computer in a chat room and getting all the current news about what had happened. "Honey, you could come home, but I don't think you will even be able to get on Fort Bragg. Everything is shut right down!" I said

"It's okay Mom, really. Keep me posted on what is going on with you and Dad, okay?" he said. That's just like him, I thought, being so strong. I was so lucky to have such wonderful kids. "I love you, Mom".

"I love you more than you know, Ian." I had said.

I truly was just a few minutes away from the Red Cross Station. I grabbed my purse, checked to make sure my keys were there and patted down a few straggly hairs as I checked myself in the mirror and then walked out the door to my car.

The Station was located on Macomb Street, four blocks from my home on Pelham Drive. Today, September 11th was the only day for the next several that I would be able to drive anywhere, even on post. After the 11th, all the roads leading anywhere were blocked.

"What, were you in the car when you called me?" Kathy teased as I walked in the back door of the Red Cross Station.

"What can I do, Kathy?" I asked. "I really so want to help in any way I can. I don't want to be a bother and I don't want you to babysit me, just give me a task, please?"

"Jane, you are one of our advisors, this isn't in your job description you know?" she stated. "But if you are serious, please answer the phones. I have several people doing that already and it would help with their loads if you would work with them. People from everywhere want to donate. This is what you need to say."

She handed me a paper telling me the process that donors would need to go through. I could handle that easily. She gave me an empty office and then hurriedly left as two people next to me were vying for her time and I could tell by the look on her face that she was already on to the next task.

Carolyn, the volunteer station manager and my dear friend,

31

poked her head in the door and said "Jane, oh this is just great! I am so glad you are here! I should have called you, forgive me! Has Kathy given you something to do? She didn't just stick you in here, did she?"

The phone began to ring, and I held up my hand to Carolyn and mouthed the words "wait a minute, I want to talk to you after this call"

Carolyn and I had become friends over the past several months and it was always a pleasure to see her cheerful face. After I got off the phone, I turned to her and said. "Don't worry Carolyn, Kathy found me a task. She got tired of me calling in and tying up the phone lines so she suggested I come down here to work. Believe me, I want to be here. Sitting at home and watching the news and worrying, wasn't doing me any good. I've been a wreck! How are you dealing with all of this?"

"I guess okay, who knows? We have been in crisis mode here and I haven't even had much of a chance to think about it all. I don't want to right now, as I know when I do, I will be a basket case. It's best just to keep me busy so my mind stays focused, you know?" she asked.

"I sure do! I'll let you get back to work. I'm so glad you are here too!" I said cheerfully.

The phone was quiet, for how long, who knew. I stared at it, pondering if I should give Gary another call. I decided not to, as my last conversation with him was very brief. He was being inundated with many tasks and he didn't need me chatting with him now. We both cried into the phone when we finally heard each other's voices and said, "I love you!" Tears began to well up in my eyes remembering this. I knew that I would not be seeing him tonight until very, very late.

The phone rang "This is Jane Davis at Fort Bragg Red Cross Station, how can I help you today?"

32

"What can I do to help, I want to donate something, I don't have much, but I have to do something!" the anxious woman on the other end of the phone stated.

I calmly gave her the information she needed to she could make her donation and thanked her repeatedly for her kind gesture. That scenario kept going all afternoon. I have no idea how many phone calls I took that but they were coming fast and furious. I was so proud to be part of such an amazing organization. The American Red Cross was everything I believed in, helping those in times of need. I had, for years, been part of Red Cross at the very local level, on the military installations. I knew that Red Cross was huge and I kept thinking, *I want to be part of the bigger picture. How can I do this? How can I make an impact on a bigger level?*

The day progressed and the time got away from us all. I felt like I answered hundreds of calls, everyone wanted to help in any way they could. At about 6:00 in the evening Kathy poked her head in the door and said, "Are you really still here? Go home! I'm closing up the place. We can do the same thing tomorrow, okay? Can you come in tomorrow? You were a huge help so I definitely can use you again!"

"Oh, of course I'll be back, you can count on me. Hey, Kathy can I ask you a quick question? What else can I do, you know, at a bigger level, like volunteering at the national level?" I asked.

"Let me give that some thought, Jane and I will get back to you on that," she said running her hands through her hair. "I know how you are feeling; you just want to do more, right? I will think about it tonight and get back to you when I see you in the morning."

"Thanks Kath, I appreciate it. Be careful on your bike, okay? I can't believe you drove your Harley in today!"

I teased.

"That's me, livin' on the edge!" She smiled, held the door for me and we both walked out.

There was an eerie silence on post, I noticed as I made my way to my car. It was as if everyone wanted to shut themselves up in their homes to ward off all of the negativity in the world. I shuddered.

My phone was ringing when I got home. "Where have you been, Mom? I've been so worried" Elizabeth exclaimed.

"Darn, I forgot to tell you as it happened so quickly. I went to volunteer at the Red Cross Station answering phones for the afternoon." I said.

"Oh, that's a relief!" Liz sighed. "I've just been so worried, my mind has been wandering all over the place and I just needed to know you are okay".

"Honey, we talked this afternoon" I said, while glancing at the phone and seeing 15 messages on it. "I really want to talk, can I call you back? I have loads of messages on my answering machine".

"As long as I know you are okay, I'm fine. Call me when you get a free minute," she said. "I'm feeding JT and waiting for James to get home".

"Okay, I'll give you a call in a bit, I promise!" I said.

I went to the task of checking the voicemail. My Mom had called twice, my sister once, Ian called twice, Elizabeth three times and Gary called just to tell me he loved me and that he would be very late as he was over at the headquarters trying to figure out logistics to keep the hospital open and the ambulances running since the post was locked down. There were several calls from friends just checking to make sure I was okay and the rest of the calls were about our Medical Wives Coffee that we were to have that evening, all knowing that it was canceled, but just wanting to chat about it.

I knew that I needed to call everyone back, but I just sat there by the phone and closed my eyes. Tears began to well up. My mind just would not turn off. What the hell had happened to our country? How many lives were lost today? The towers had fallen, who knows how many people were inside. Oh God, before the towers fell, people were jumping out the windows to their deaths! The Pentagon had taken a major hit. Our country had changed today; I knew that, nothing would ever be the same again. What could I do, one little person in the whole scheme of things. I felt so very helpless.

The phone ringing snapped me back to reality. "Hey Jane, how are you holding up? I called before, did you get it? " It was Barb on the phone.

"No, I didn't get your message as I just walked in the door from helping at Red Cross," I said.

"What are you doing this evening? Do you have time to get together with all of us from the running group? We are meeting at Dave's house", she said out of breath.

"Barb, really, are you really all getting together tonight? What's up?" I asked incredulously.

"Well it's like this, who knows when we will have this opportunity again to do this with all of the horrific stuff going on. Our spouses are all stressed and will be working who knows how long! You know all of us in the running group are like family to each other and we thought this might be the only time we have to console each other. What do you think? Dave is planning on making his *Dark and Stormy's* he has been talking so much about!" She exclaimed. "So what do you think? Are you in?"

"How can I pass up a Dark and Stormy?" I joked. "I'll be there, when are we meeting?"

"We are meeting at his house at around 7:00, in just a few minutes, does that give you enough time?" she asked.

"I have a lot of calls to answer as I was gone all afternoon," I said.

"We all have a lot of calls, Jane. Let them go and come on over, please? It might be our only opportunity", she pleaded. How right she was as it ended up being our only opportunity.

"Okay!" I said. "Let me just feed and let Womack (our Golden Retriever) and Princess (our Yorkie) out and I will be on over. See you in about 10-15 minutes".

"Cell phones are left at the door," Dave said after giving me a big hug as I walked in the door to his home. "None of us are available to ANYONE! This is our night, our Iron Mike Runners night and it's probably our only night, so Jane, hand it over", he said holding out a basket for me to drop it in.

Everyone gave a cheer as I deposited my phone in with everyone else's. "For one deposited cell phone, one deserves a Dark and Stormy!" he said as he handed the drink to me.

"I know we should talk about the horrific events that happened today," Dave lamented, but for tonight can we just not do it, at least for a little while? It's not that I don't care, as you know I do, but we have been trying to cope with it all day long and I don't know about you, but I need a break from it even if it is ever so brief. We have all been inundated today, each and every one of us, and this is just one of the many days to come. In saying that everyone, please raise your glasses, I am toasting to the many lost souls, the lives that abruptly changed this morning. What a terrible time this is in our nation's history. Let us remain strong and persevere through whatever may be coming our nation's way."

We all toasted, tears rolling down most of our faces. Barb then said, "Here's to us and the sanctity of our friendship!" It lightened the mood, just what we needed.

The mood in the room was tentative at best. We were trying the impossible, trying to forget the events of the day. At times, it appeared to be working and then a cell phone would ring from the basket and we would all turn to look. "Nobody answer it, do you hear me? Step away from the basket!" Barb warned. "We don't need no stinkin' cell phones… you hear me?" We all laughed.

This was what we needed, the friendship, and camaraderie. I felt so lucky to have these wonderful people in my life. We all knew to grasp at this evening, to cherish it for what it was. Tomorrow would come all too soon and the realities would come flooding back to us… all too quickly.

I retrieved my cell phone from the basket as we all did when we said our goodbyes that evening. Little did I know that would be the last time I would have the chance socialize with all of them together. Life really was not the same after that day.

There were only five missed calls on my cell phone, three from Ian, one from my sister and one from Elizabeth. I dialed Ian's number on the way to my car. "Mom, are you okay? I've been calling and calling!"

"I'm sorry Ian, it's been crazy here and I haven't had much time. How are you holding up with all of this news?" I asked.

"This is just crazy, it makes no sense. Who would do such a thing?" he exclaimed.

"I wish I was there in Raleigh with you," I said. "You aren't that far away but it might as well be across the ocean as this post is shut down tight!"

"I know Mom, I wish that I was with you too, I really do. Liz and I are keeping in touch too and if school is closed again tomorrow, I'm going over to be with her, James and JT."

"Oh that would be fantastic!" I exclaimed. "You guys need to be with each other!"

We said our goodbyes. I looked at my watch 10:30, too late to call my sister. I would call her in the morning. I dialed Elizabeth.

"Forget about me, Mom?" Liz teased.

"No, friends invited me to get together at Dave's house. We sat around and talked and drank. It was so nice. Who knows when we will get that chance again?"

"I'm glad you did that, you needed that! I was just worried. You said you would call me back in a few minutes and that was around 6:30 pm," she said.

"I am fine, just exhausted. I hope your Dad is home, though I doubt it."

"He's still at work, really? God, that's awful!"

"He's a commander, Liz, and that is how it goes when you are in a position like that. I expected as much. I'm sure the next several days will be very similar." I explained.

"Well I hope you guys get some rest," she said. We said our goodbyes and promised to chat again in the morning.

I walked in the front door, no Gary, but was greeted by Womack and Princess wagging their tails. *Oh to have a dog's life with not a care in the world other than being happy to see your family,* I thought. I bent down and scratched behind their ears. "Who's my good boy, who makes his Mommy so happy?" I asked Womack and then gave him a big hug. Princess licked my face over and over. It was so nice to feel their unconditional love. Womack seemed to know something was up as he just leaned into the hug and stayed there. After a couple of minutes, I got up, grabbed their leashes and took them for their nightly walk. We all needed the fresh air.

We walked around the parade field pausing frequently so both dogs could sniff almost every square inch. I didn't mind. The walk refreshed me and gave me some time to think, to go back through the day. *What can I do?* I thought. *I need to do more. This just isn't enough, and I feel a need and I have to help. I'll talk to Kathy tomorrow and maybe she can figure out what I can do. I want to go and it doesn't matter where, New York, DC, Pennsylvania. All I know is I've got to!* It was the first time that day that I had over five minutes to myself to just think, to process all that happened. I made the determination that there was no way I could ever process what took place. I would just have to try daily to make some sense of this.

As I rounded the corner to my house, Gary was getting out of his car. "Well, finally!" I said and ran to him and gave him a hug. I didn't want to let go, I wanted to hold him forever. Of course, the dogs wouldn't let me and they were jumping and clambering to be with their daddy.

"Oh, Jane I am just exhausted" Gary said as we entered the house. "I know it is going to be like this for quite a while, but I know I can do it. How have things gone today for you? I'm sure you stayed busy and probably solved all the problems of the world, my volunteer extraordinaire!"

"I wish!" I sighed. "I've talked to all of the family, friends, and then some. Oh, and I spent the afternoon at Red Cross answering the phone lines. It was crazy! Then I went over to Dave's house with all the running group people. We consoled each other as much as we could. What the hell is going on Gary? I just cannot grasp the enormity of it. None of this makes any sense to me. Is our country at war? Who would do such a thing and kill innocent people?"

"Well, life has changed as we know it," Gary said as he sat down on the living room sofa.

"Can I get you something to eat?" I asked.

"I think I'm just too tired. I know, hard to believe, right. I always eat when I'm stressed" he joked. "I had a bite to eat at the hospital a few hours ago, so I'm okay, though a beer sounds pretty good right now. I'll get it; you don't have to, as you have been working hard all day too."

"I don't mind at all," I said. "I will get one too and we can just sit here and talk."

I grabbed two cold Yuenglings from the refrigerator and walked back to the couch and handed one to Gary. I stood there, looking down at him. His head was in his hands and he was just staring at some non-descript spot on the floor. I said, "I can't watch the television anymore tonight so let's just talk. You know, I'm afraid I won't be able to sleep, as I'll just keep seeing those people jumping from the towers and then, oh my God, I will see the towers falling and all those lives lost!" I started to cry.

He pulled me down to the couch and placed his hand under my chin and tilted my face to meet his. His kiss was warm and tender. I didn't want to let go. We needed each other and it felt so right to have him there, my husband, my best friend. We lost ourselves in each other's embrace and our tears began and kept flowing and flowing.

CHAPTER 6

Preparation

"Jane, I need your help," Kathy said breathlessly into her cell phone.

"Sure, where are you, there's lots of background noise?" I asked.

"I'm waiting in the freaking long line to get on Post! All of us that live off-Post have to go through hell and back to get on, now that this disaster has happened. So you have a key to the Red Cross Station, don't you?" she asked. "You are one of the few that lives on Post, all of the rest of us have to try to make it through this mess. Can you get the doors unlocked? What a miserable day!"

"Absolutely, Kath, I'm right on it and should get there in less than fifteen minutes. Will that be okay?"

"It will be outstanding. Why did I ride my bike in today? This is the pits and it may be hours before I get there. They are really being careful who they let on this Post. I mean, I get it as we have had a major crisis here in our country, but really?" she asked. "I know, I know! We are one of the big military facilities in this country and they want to be sure that no one is going to come in and do us harm, I get it, but it freaking drives me crazy waiting… I'm not a patient person!"

"No worries, Kathy, I'm right there for you. I told you I would do whatever I could do to help!" I reminded her.

"When I get there, we will talk about your next step in this disaster process. I've been doing some thinking about it. I need to make some phone calls to make sure, but I think I know the where-to-go from here," she informed me.

"Thanks Kathy for giving it some thought as I know you have a lot on your mind right now and you don't need to be worrying about me!"

"Oh hell, there is so much to worry about it is ridiculous, so why not one more? Let me get off the phone and move my bike a quarter of an inch forward... damn. Plus I want you to get in there and open up the doors!" she laughed.

"I'm on it. See you soon, I hope!" I hung up the phone and raced through the house in search of the keys.

Mack and Princess just stared at me, like I was the tennis ball in a tennis match. Back and forth, back and forth... *Think Jane! Where were you last time you needed those keys? THINK!* As if in a vision I saw them taking shape. *That's right, in the green purse! I remember now, that's the purse I was using when we had our last Red Cross Station meeting. I had to unlock the building that day too.* Wow, it seemed like an eon ago, but it was only just a week before. I scrambled up the stairs and into the bedroom closet, praying to myself that my 'vision' was right on. *Come on green purse, where are you?* I could hear Gary in my mind teasing me. "Why does anyone need so many purses?" I wish I knew but it is one of my downfalls! *Ahh, there it is hiding under my jacket! Please keys, be there! Voila... I'm a genius!*

With keys in hand, I hurried down the stairs and saw two sad dogs staring at me. While grabbing the dog leashes I leaned down to rub Mack's ears. Princess came running over to get in on the attention she felt she so rightly deserved. "Come on kiddos; let me take you for a short walk. Sorry you are being so neglected right now! Who knows how long this will last!"

A short fifteen minutes later, I was opening up the Red Cross Station at Fort Bragg. *Now what? I thought to myself. What the heck am I supposed to do?* I was settled in just in time, the first phone call was coming in. I was busy in phone conversation and looked up to see Carolyn poking her head in the doorway. I mouthed the words "Give me five minutes!" to her and finished up my conversation.

"Carolyn, I'm so glad you are here! How did you get in so quickly?" I said while giving my dear friend a well-deserved hug.

"Kathy called me on my cell phone, while I was waiting in line at the gate. I guess I went to the right gate on Post as I only had a 45 minute wait. I don't know if Kathy will make it in, the line is so long! She told me not to worry though as she said that you were opening the Station up. Thank you!" she said in her beautiful southern drawl. I could listen to her all day! Carolyn was the volunteer side of Kathy. Kathy was the Station Manager and Carolyn, her counterpart.

"I'm just delighted you are here!" I gushed. "I was afraid I would be here alone all day! Did you know that even the back streets on Post are closed? I had to walk over here… not that it was a big deal, only a ten minute walk!"

"You and I can handle it, but don't worry I know others are on their way here too so we won't be alone" she said. "There go the phones again. I'll take this one okay?"

The hours flew by and we eventually had five of us volunteering in the Station handling whatever came our way. Kathy kept calling with updates on how far she had advanced in the long line to get on Post. Debbie, from my running group called me and asked if they, the running group, could get some lunch together for us in the Station. We were so grateful that they even thought of us and were ravenous by the time the food arrived.

As it turned out, Kathy finally gave up at 3:00 and turned around to go home. That was the story with everyone all over Post. Everyone was in a long line, some waiting over eight hours, coming in to their duty assignment, signing in and then turning around to go home.

We locked the doors at 6:00 pm, exhausted, knowing that tomorrow, Thursday, would be more of the same. It was good for me though, as I could barely stand being at home and watching the news. It was a constant on the news channels, speculation of which terrorist group had done this to our country. Was Osama bin Laden in charge of this heinous act on American soil? The questions and concerns were rampant. I wanted to do more! This was killing me; I needed to help in a bigger way!

"I've got your answer," Kathy said, smiling at me as she walked in to the Station on Thursday morning.

"Hey, you made it!" I grinned. "Not bad today, you are only two hours late! I'll forgive you. Did you leave the motorcycle at home?"

"Ha-ha... yes I did. Traffic ran smoother today and the line was... hey, only two hours long to get on Post! What an amazing event! Who would think that two hours is something to be pleased about?" she laughed.

"So what do you think I can do, Kathy?" I anxiously asked.

"I've got to make some phone calls to the Fayetteville Red Cross, the Highlands Chapter. They will need to get you trained and we need to see when the next set of classes is. Jane it may be a while before you can get in all the classes you will need, before you are certified in Disaster Services and meet all the criteria", she informed me.

"Wow, I had no idea!" I commented. "I just never realized that I had to take classes. It makes sense! Well, I am ready to take them right away, the sooner the better!"

"It may take me a while to get this figured out as I have a lot of other stuff going on today, as you can only imagine. I can't believe I couldn't get in here yesterday. I was just so frustrated waiting in the line from hell!" she groaned.

"I'll wait…and try to be patient," I said smiling.

"I know you Jane, you are not a patient woman, like me, but give me a bit of time and I'll find you and let you know" she said, lightly touching my arm. "Go find a phone to answer in the mean time!"

I was amazed that the number of phone calls had not changed and we all were still so busy at the Red Cross Station. Again, the day flew by.

Kathy entered the office in the mid-afternoon, smiling broadly. "You are in major luck kiddo. The chapter has jumped on this and has set up several disaster training classes. I think there must be some other nurses wanting to go so they are also setting up a Disaster Health Services class."

"When?" I asked.

"Oh, sorry" she said. "Training starts this Saturday! It looks like you will be able to get all of your training in a week's time! That is really unusual, but I guess this is an unusual time. I'm so glad that the chapter stepped up to the plate to make this happen."

I was ecstatic! I was really going to get trained and really going to be able to go and help out! I jumped up from behind my desk and threw my arms around her. "Thank you so much!"

"You are very welcome. I'm glad I could find this out for you. I've never seen anyone quite so eager to get involved as you!" she laughed.

"I'll make you proud, Kathy, I promise you that!" I told her.

Training was intense and there were many forms to fill out so I would be DSHR certified, Disaster Services Human Resources. Once the initial training was completed, I would be able to go to any national disaster. Everyone was very helpful and positive and wanted to see this happen for me. I was amazed by their eagerness to help me. Once the training was completed, the only thing I could do was wait, wait for the National Headquarters of American Red Cross to complete the paperwork and give me the approval.

I was like a caged lion, waiting and waiting. It had been well over two and a half weeks since the disaster, training was complete, all the paperwork turned in. Waiting for the word was almost impossible. I started to pack, as I needed something to do. I learned in my training how to pack and always be prepared for a disaster, so I figured it was time to put what I learned to work.

The acceptance letter finally arrived in early October, with my DSHR registration. I would be going to New York City. Where in New York I had no idea, but at least I had a general location. I had three days to get everything together. They gave me the phone number to call for my flight to New York. All of this was paid by the generous donations made to the Red Cross. I called the number and told the very sweet lady on the phone that I would be traveling from Fayetteville, North Carolina to New York City. These arrangements were quickly made. I should have followed up a bit more.

Gary dropped me at the airport on October 4th and after a tearful goodbye, I headed into the airport to the ticket counter. No one was there. I mean, NO one! I panicked. Was I late, had I missed my flight? I reached into my carry-on bag and grabbed my paperwork. No, this WAS the right day. What was going on?

"Excuse me," I said to an agent walking by. "I was told that there was a flight to New York City today. Nobody is at the counter!"

"Let me check for you, sweetie. What time is your flight?"

She asked in her Fayetteville drawl. "Well, we don't have any flights the rest of the day, are you sure you were to go today? What's your flight number?"

I handed her my information and she went to the computer and entered my information in. "Well, I see what the problem is. Whoever booked this for you put in Fayetteville, Arkansas!" she said laughing.

I was devastated, how could that be? "I told her North Carolina! Oh no! My ride is on his way back to Fort Bragg!" I yelped. "Are you sure there are no other flights today?"

"We have one tomorrow early afternoon. Why don't you give them a call and see if they can get it changed for you." She suggested.

"First I'll call my husband and tell him he has me for one more day!" I laughed.

"Were you going to New York to help with the disaster?" she asked.

"That's what I'm trying to do! Thanks for all of your help. I'll probably see you again tomorrow!" I grinned.

As luck would have it, I was able to reach Gary before he got too far away from the airport. I also got in touch with the folks about my flight to New York. We all got a good laugh about it and I was booked for the following day. I was sad that the trip was postponed by one day, but really, it was just ONE day and I would get there soon enough.

CHAPTER 7

Arrival

What have I done? I thought as my plane landed in New York City. Thoughts were racing through my brain; *I have left my family and friends, the comfort of my home and am now off in a city where I know no one. I am alone! What made me think that I could do this? Travel off because someone needed help. What kind of help can I give?* I kept second-guessing myself over and over. I wanted to turn and run, but knew deep in my heart I had to press on.

I made my way to the luggage carousel and grabbed my tiny suitcase. We were told to pack light, just the essentials, as we would be moving frequently. I don't think I have ever packed 'light' in my life, but I guess there is always a first time!

I glanced around, noticed several people, and immediately knew I would be okay. Each was quite identifiable by the Red Cross T-shirts they wore. I sauntered over to a pleasant looking 60ish year old woman and asked her, "Are you here to volunteer for the disaster?"

She peered down at me and smiling said, "Are you as nervous as I am?"

I let out an audible sigh and we both looked at each other and broke into laughter.

"Hey Sarah, did you find another volunteer?" came a big booming voice behind me. I turned to see a very large man striding his way over to where we were standing.

"Hi, I'm Sarah, as you probably guessed by now!" she said.

"And I am Jim, her better half," he bellowed as he put his arm around his wife. "Is there anyone you brought with you?"

"No, it's just me. Hi, I'm Jane. I was told to take

this flight and then once I got here to call to the main Headquarters. Is that what we need to do next?" I asked, trying to make my voice appear stronger and not look as scared as I felt.

"That's the plan. Is this your first disaster?" Sarah asked.

"That it is, is it that obvious?" I joked.

"No it isn't, just a guess. You actually look pretty confident!" Sarah grinned. "I think we will be seeing a lot of first time volunteers here for this disaster. Jim and I have been doing Red Cross disasters since we retired four years ago. I guess this must be about our sixth one, right Jim?"

"It's our seventh one, sweetie. How soon you forget!" Jim teased. "We might as well round up everyone here and just make one phone call," he suggested. "I'll go grab the other folks. It looks like there are about eight of us Red Crossers here."

Before long we were all told to head to our hotels, mine being Howard Johnson's, all of us being put up throughout Midtown Manhattan. We, except for the couples, were assigned in separate hotels. Wherever there were hotel openings Red Cross took advantage of it. I didn't realize that we would be staying in hotels, I just assumed we would be staying in dorm-like settings. I then assumed that I would be sharing a room with another 'Red Crosser.' I was told that due to the difficult assignment that we each needed our own 'down time'. I was flabbergasted.

The next day we were told to go to Red Cross Headquarters to find out where our assigned locations would be. Try to get a good night's sleep. Ha! We were told to arrive at Headquarters by 9:00 a.m. and be prepared to be there for most of the day. We would be receiving our assignments, and our ID passes, our Red Cross aprons and hard hats (if going to Ground Zero) and finalizing the rest of our training. Red Cross was very thorough on their processing of disaster volunteers.

I could barely sleep. The TV was left on all night for background noise. I wrote in my journal, read a book, just tried to find anything possible to distract me. I felt alone, vulnerable in this big city. I wasn't used to the cacophony outside my window, horns blaring in the middle of the night! Finally, around 3:00 in the morning, I fell asleep.

The alarm went off a short three and a half hours later, so much for that good night's sleep! There was no use hanging around in bed, time was wasting. I had to shower, get my papers together and figure out how to get to the Headquarters. I had been to Manhattan several times before, but never felt very confident getting around the city. That would quickly change!

I arrived at Red Cross HQ just shy of 8:30, eager to get in-processed and learn where I would be headed to start with my volunteering. The lines were already forming. I guess I didn't know what to expect, but there was at least a hundred people already with more arriving as time went on. This disaster had caused a plethora of volunteers to come to the city; it was as if it was a pilgrimage. They were everywhere! I can't imagine how many volunteers they processed in every day!

After attending all of my training , the last two steps were to find out the location I would be volunteering and then receive my ID badge and find out if I had Ground Zero access or not. I entered Disaster Health Services and waited in a long line. I overheard the same story repeatedly. "Can I work at Ground Zero?" was the constant mantra. I listened and thought to myself, this is not what to ask for as I could see that the HQ officers were tired of hearing it. "Now Debbie, not everyone can go to Ground Zero, we have many locations around the city that need a huge amount of help. We have to work with the families too and need help at the piers assisting in the family process," I heard the head nurse, Jean say.

"Hi, I'm Jane, coming in from Fort Bragg, North Carolina," I said to Jean and reached out to shake her hand.

"Hi Jane, I'm Jean. It is a pleasure to meet you," she said pointing down at a paper in front of her. "Ah, here you are on the list. Tell me what y'all are thinking you might want to do?" Jean drawled, with her thick Louisiana accent.

"Well Jean, I am very new to this as this is my first disaster. I know everyone wants to go to Ground Zero, but please feel free to put me wherever you think my skills will be of the most help," I said.

"Tell me a bit about you," she asked. "What have you been doing at Fort Bragg?"

I told her about the volunteering I had been doing with military families, to include being an advisor to the Red Cross Station, the leadership roles that I had been holding, and my nursing experiences over the past several years. "With my traveling all around the world, as my husband is with the military, my life has taken many twists and turns, as has my career," I chimed in.

"I'm impressed!" she grinned. "I think you could be a huge asset and would like you to be assigned to one of the First Aid stations within the Ground Zero perimeter."

I looked at her with sheer amazement as I had just seen her tell the last three nurses signing in that Ground Zero was off limits to them. "I would be honored and I promise, Jean, I won't let you down!" I exclaimed.

"I'm holding you to that" she chuckled. "Now take this paper that states you will have Ground Zero access to the ID station. I'd like you to start tomorrow. You will be going to the school that is located about two blocks from the pile."

"The pile?" I asked.

"That is the name everyone has given the Ground Zero site," she stated, shaking her head with genuine sadness.

"How will I know where to go?" I asked.

"Once you get off the subway, head down Chambers until you see the school, PS 89, with the giant American Flag on it. That's it! Now you will have the evening shift so you don't need to be there until 3:00. You are looking mighty tired Jane; I see the circles under your eyes. Go get that ID, grab some food here in the cafeteria, and head back to your hotel. You need to rest up, as it will be a long day tomorrow. The first day always is. It is emotionally exhausting."

I wanted to hug her to thank her. She was such a warm and helpful individual. I found out later that you either loved or hated her, most people thinking the latter. But we had bonded and I already felt such closeness to her. That would continue throughout my tenure. Instead, I reached out and shook her hand. "It's such a pleasure to meet you Jean," I warmly said.

You will know where the building is once you see the flag, I kept repeating to myself as I headed for the subway to take me to Chambers Street the next day. The streets in Midtown were noisy, typical of New York City. Taxis were honking, showing their usual impatience. If one didn't know any better, it would be hard to notice that there was a major disaster going on just a short distance south of where I stood. The only major difference I could see was the patriotism that had taken over the city. Flags were flying everywhere and I mean everywhere. Almost every single building displayed an American flag. I looked up and saw the fluttering of hundreds of flags. It made me smile and it made me sad.

I found the subway train that I needed to take and left

58

the noisy city behind me. There were only a few of us left on the subway by the time we arrived at Chambers. From the minute I stepped off the subway, I sensed a palpable difference. I just couldn't pinpoint what it was, it seemed haunting but maybe it was just my imagination, my own fears. I climbed the stairs and stepped into the light of day, though daylight isn't the word I would use to describe how it appeared to me. It was as if I had gone from color (Midtown) to black and white. The buildings and surrounding streets cast a gray foreboding backdrop. There were very few individuals on the streets but the ones that were there appeared to be talking in hushed tones. It was as if everyone was in church and keeping their words soft and quiet. This startled me, as it was such a stark contrast to Midtown. How strange that just a short distance away could be so full of life.

The subway stop was in close proximity to City Hall. *Great, at least I have a landmark*, I thought. *Travel down Chambers until you see the building with the big American Flag,* I kept saying to myself. I had reviewed the map over and over the night before and thankfully, I have a pretty good sense of direction. *If I keep walking, I should see the World Trade Center site to my left.*

I made my way to the intersection of Chambers and Church Street, just two blocks from where I exited the subway. I stopped, watching a small group of people at the corner just staring out in the distance to a site I couldn't see from where I stood. I was pretty confident I knew what they were seeing, Ground Zero. There was such a profound grief and sadness on their faces. A cold chill raced through me while watching them. With trepidation, I made my way over to Church Street. *There is no turning back Jane, this is it. You have to go take a look, take it all in before you start volunteering.*

Turning the corner, I halted my step at the Church Street intersection. I stared incredulously at the confusion directly in front of me, my mouth dropped. I tried to focus my eyes, grasp at reality as to what lay before me, such devastation. There was an inordinate amount of debris, piles of it! Now it became clear to me why Jean told me that Ground Zero was called "The pile". These were enormous piles, slabs of concrete, holding no definition as to what they originally were. Some sections of the buildings were still partially standing, while others were completely unrecognizable. There, straight ahead and to my right, stood what was left of a parking garage, with several cars still inside, *abandoned forever,* I assumed. The majority of the vehicles were demolished beyond recognition. *Oh my God, this is not like what I saw on TV, this is worse than anything I could ever imagine!* Little did I know what I was seeing was not the main devastation of the two trade towers but of smaller buildings that had collapsed from its wake. Tears began to well up.

Then it hit me, an overpowering intense stench. *What in the world was it?* How does one describe that burning raw pungent mixture? I really didn't want to know **what** this horrific smell was, as my mind started to wonder as to all the many possibilities of what could be mixed in with it. I immediately placed my hand over my nostrils to help clear that foreboding odor out of my head. I started shaking my head, *this can't be real, this must be some sort of dream. No this cannot be a dream, who in their right mind would dream something as dreadful as this? This is truly a nightmare!* That initial view and smell has been ingrained in my head even to this day. I'm afraid it is something I will never ever be able to eliminate from the depths of my soul.

I questioned myself for the umpteenth time, *what the heck*

am I doing here? I didn't want to take it all in; I didn't want to smell that acrid odor. I shuddered and took a tentative breath telling myself to *step away from all of the chaos.* The initial thought was to run as far as I could away from the devastation. But I knew deep down that running back to the safety and security of my hotel would not be the right plan. I had to be strong and prove to myself that this could be done; I could work at Ground Zero and even make a difference. I needed to keep moving, but in the direction of Ground Zero. I kept repeating to myself, *Just put one foot in front of the other, Jane.* It was time to begin my volunteer experience. *Hurry,* I thought. *Don't look at it; just keep your eyes focused on what is straight ahead! Look for that flag!*

The red, white and blue of our country's flag stood off in the distance. Its beauty mesmerized me. These were the only colors that I had noticed since leaving the subway. All was a blanket of gray except for this beautiful American Flag. It was shrouding my entire building! *Now I understand what Jean was telling me, this has to be it!* I found myself almost racing towards it, focusing on it alone. I was breathing heavily, but feeling so determined not to slow down, not to look back. Nothing was going to stop me, nothing! *There is a purpose for why you are here,* I thought, and that purpose and strength would see me through this country's difficult time.

I reached for the door and stepped inside.

CHAPTER 8

Early Days

I cautiously opened the glass school door, realizing that at that very moment, I was on the threshold of this disaster assignment, one that would ultimately change my life. I pushed on through and entered inside with much trepidation. While scanning the room I thought, *this doesn't look like an elementary school*! A transformation had obviously occurred at PS 89, as I did not recognize it as a school cafeteria. Several stations were set up to house the many emergency organizations that were deemed important for this disaster. This area/school had become Ground Zero's Emergency Headquarters. People were bustling around all caught up in their own concerns.

"ID please," said a sandy haired soldier from the Army National Guard.

I was caught by surprise with his statement and took a small step back. All of this was done in a split second while I was looking up at the tall and lanky young man. *Oh right*, I thought, *I needed to have access to get in to this area, and hence why I needed my special ID badge stating that I had full Ground Zero Access.*

"Forgive me, this is my first day here and I am feeling a bit flustered," I uttered, my face blushing. I grabbed for my backpack and began pawing through its contents, hurrying as to not take up too much of his time. "Ah, there it is! I forgot I needed to be wearing this!"

"Great to have you here, Miss Davis," he said reading my ID. "It looks like you are one of the Red Crossers. Don't worry about being flustered; we all were on the first day or two", he said with a grin. Are you a nurse?"

"That I am! Can you tell me where I need to be?" I asked. "They told me that there is a First Aid Station in here somewhere. There are a lot of people and I must admit I don't have a clue where I need to be going!"

"Go to the back right corner of the cafeteria, right next to where the chow line is," he said pointing. "Do you see that young guy straight ahead, sitting at that table, talking to the other guy that is balding and a bit overweight?" He gave a wave to the young man sitting at a cafeteria table that was laden with medical supplies. The young man looked up from his conversation, smiled, waved back and then began to stride over to where I was standing.

"Thanks, Sergeant Frasier," I said smiling. He glanced at me with such surprise. I could almost see the bubble form above him as he wondered how I knew his military rank. The Army life, that I was so accustomed to for most of my adult life, appeared to be paying off. I relaxed a bit as just knowing the National Guard was right there, close at hand, made me feel right at home and gave me such comfort!

"Hi, I'm Sam; you must be Jane, right?" said the fellow Red Cross worker who had finally made his way over to where I was standing. "It looks like you and I are partners on this shift."

"Nice to meet you Sam, wow, this place is quite the operation!" I exclaimed while scanning the room watching the hustle and bustle.

"Come on over to the First Aid table. We can talk better over there as it is a bit quieter." He led the way, me following behind like a scared little puppy dog. I must have had an odd look on my face as he turned to me and smiled, "Feeling a bit overwhelmed about this whole process?"

"That is an understatement!" I stated as we arrived at the table. "I guess it is pretty obvious that this is my first disaster and though I knew it would be an overwhelming feeling, I just had no idea it would impact me so quickly. And I really haven't seen anything yet!"

"So you haven't seen the Pile?" He asked, gesturing for me to take a seat. "Oh, of course not, it's all new to you. I will try to set something up so you can see it all."

"Really, we will get to see it?" I asked incredulously. "I thought we wouldn't get very close to it!"

"Do you realize how close we are to the Pile now?" he asked.

"Well, obviously pretty close as I saw some of it as I was walking here from the subway," I offered.

"You really didn't see the total damage, and you NEED to see it," he emphasized. "So you can see what the rescue/recovery workers are up against. It truly is total devastation. I don't want you to see it today, as you are already too overwhelmed. I'll work on getting something set up in the next day or two. So, on a lighter note, where are you coming from?"

"Fort Bragg, North Carolina," I said. "How about yourself?"

"L.A., er, Los Angeles, California. I have been here for over two weeks and just have a few more days left. This is just great that you are here, I can show you the ropes before I head out of here on Friday."

"Really, you are leaving this Friday?" I asked.

"Yup, the assignments are only for three weeks and I need to get back as I am an EMT and they are holding my position for me there. I must admit it, I don't want to go back yet as I have really been enjoying my time here. I see that look on your face," he smirked, "you must think I have lost a screw or something as how could I enjoy being here, right?"

"As a matter of fact, that thought did cross my mind," I admitted. "What the heck could be enjoyable about this?" I said while glancing around the room.

"You'll find that the people are awesome, well not just only in PS 89 but everyone you meet that is involved with this mega-operation. We are all here for the same purpose and it really has drawn us all together into a close family-like atmosphere. I didn't believe that I could get so close to so many of these people in such a short period of time, but it is as if time stands still and we have known each other all of our lives!" He stopped talking, made a deep sigh while glancing around the room. "Sorry to go on and on, you will see, and I know by the time you leave you will be feeling the same way that I am."

"I really like your positive attitude, Sam. I'm so impressed. I can see that this has left a huge impression on you!" I grinned. "How about you show me around this cafeteria and the First Aid Station so I know what I need to be doing and I know where things are located."

I found out that the First Aid Station appeared to be the 'hang-out' for just about everyone. People seemed to feel comfortable coming over and just sitting down and visiting. Mostly we were taking care of those that were assigned to this Emergency HQ location in the school, but occasionally we would see the workers from the Ground Zero site (the Pile). Those workers usually went to a building that was just a block away, called the Respite Center. I would eventually become quite familiar with the Respite Center during my volunteer time at Ground Zero. We also took care of several staff members from the school, which mostly consisted of the maintenance crew. These lovely souls had such pride in their school and didn't want to have anything happen to it. I would spend many evenings chatting with just about everyone associated with this building.

I was sitting alone at the table; Sam was a short distance

away, talking to someone and was in deep conversation. A man, approximately in his mid 50's, sauntered over to my table and pulled a chair over to sit down. "So you are the new nurse, huh?"

"Yep, that would be me. Hi, I'm Jane. Who are you?"

"Bob," he lazily said while fiddling with a package of gauze bandages. "I work for FEMA and I'm just waiting for the dinner line to open up. Did Sam tell you about our great food here?"

I wanted to grab that package out of his hand, so he wouldn't contaminate the contents, but decided that might not be a good first impression. "No, I haven't heard about the food, what's the deal with it. Who is it for?"

He looked over at the food area and set down the gauze, reaching for a pencil. I slowly reached out, grabbed the gauze and placed it on my lap. I think I did it pretty covertly so he wouldn't notice I had removed it. As luck would have it, my surreptitious activities were oblivious to him.

"Anyone here in the building," he said. "They have an amazing group of people cooking the food, in fact all the areas around here at Ground Zero have great food, and you know the other Respite Centers too. Did you know that they have chefs from many restaurants all over the city coming in and volunteering their time to feed us all?"

"No, I had no idea about that," I said. "How expensive are these meals?"

"Oh, you ARE a newbie," he scoffed. "They are free while you are working and some of the bigger places, like the Respite Centers, are always open serving some sort of meal, or snack. I do know that the Red Crossers are in charge of the delivering of the meals, not the nurses."

"Yeah, they are part of the Red Cross group called, Mass Care," I said. "I just learned about them when I went through my disaster training. I hear that they do an amazing job getting food out to everyone during disasters. It's quite an organization that Red Cross operates!"

"Well the lines just opened, come on up with me and I will introduce you to the staff that feeds us these great meals!" he said.

We just finished eating our hearty meal. "This is just an amazing meal!" I said incredulously. "I'm just having a hard time with the concept of it. I know I will get used to this, but dang this is pretty darn incredible!"

"Jane, please stop feeling guilty! You can't keep doing that!" Sam teased. We were sitting at an open cafeteria table, directly next to our First Aid Station so we could keep an eye on any visitors that might need some care. I had been feeling uncomfortable taking the food and not paying for it. It was an odd concept for me to get used to. "They want to feed us, Jane, they really do".

We had a few people come by that evening in the need of bandages, but the illness du jour seemed to be the headache and most were in need of just a few aspirin.

"It's almost time to head back to our hotels," Sam said at around 11:45. We have to head out and wait for our busses. Don't take the subway, okay? Not at night, it's a bit dangerous at this time. Daytime is fine, remember that!"

I nodded in agreement. I was so glad he was there to show me the ropes. "Tomorrow, if we can get someone to watch our station, I'm gonna see if we can get that tour of Ground Zero and then Respite Center One," he told me.

"Really? You think I am ready for it?"

"No one is ready for it, you will see tomorrow, but I think we can get that tour, or at least we can try, okay? I know we can at least get to the Respite Center as we have our badges. We should try to have dinner while we are there. So, how are you feeling after your first day?" he grinned.

"Exhausted," I exclaimed, "I don't feel like I really did tons of work, but this is all so new to me, I guess I'm just still feeling a bit overwhelmed!"

"Hah… I get it; I felt the exact same way when I got here. It's just a mental overload," he agreed. "Get a good night's sleep. You will still feel wiped out for several more days. Being here just can be exhausting. Wait till you see the Pile and the work that goes on there, you will really get a mental overdose seeing that!"

"I know that tonight I will sleep like a baby, I was too keyed up last night to get any sort of semblance of restful sleep. The only thing I plan on doing is writing in my journal and then getting some much needed sleep, I promise!"

We waited for our busses to take us back to our hotels, each one heading to their individual routes in midtown with several hotel drop-off locations.

We all got on our specific bus and exited the perimeter of Ground Zero. I was so caught up in my thoughts of the evening that I barely heard the background noise. It kept getting louder and pretty soon I began to hear yelling and cheering in the street about a block from the site. I glanced out the window and there on a street corner were several people, maybe 15 or so. They have been standing on the street corner ever since the incident on 11 September, standing out there with banners and flags waving, asking everyone to honk for the USA! I was flabbergasted. I realized that they were thanking us for coming to their city to help with the disaster. I was blown away! I would soon find out that these individuals would be on our route at the same spot every single night cheering us on. Tears filled my eyes as I sat there staring out at them. I was in awe, overwhelmed and very tired, waving in return at those lovely crazy souls.

This letter was given to me by some of those very special people.

A letter to the rescue workers

So many of you deny that you are heroes saying you are just doing your jobs.

Well, okay, maybe it's not heroic to have chosen your profession. Maybe it's not heroic to love that job. Maybe it's not heroic to feel the rush of adrenaline when the call for help comes in.

BUT, it is heroic that you keep your promise and come when called. You don't stop to consider what dangers may be waiting for you. You don't stop to analyze how hard the job will be. You just come ready to do whatever needs to be done.

Even now when your hearts are breaking and your spirits are empty, you still allow us to lean on you and to ask you to rescue us from that pit of hell.

No one could ever be prepared, no matter how hard they trained, to do the job we are counting on you to do, a job none of us could possible face ourselves. No compassionate human being should ever have to see the things you are seeing. And yet you are still there trying to bring back to us loved ones, co-workers, fellow Americans, fellow human beings.

For this, YES you are truly HEROES and will always be in our hearts! THANK YOU!

"Sixteen acres of devastation" were the words blaring in my ears the next morning as I was waking up. I had fallen asleep with the television on as the background noise helped and didn't make me feel quite so lonely. *Wait, what did they just say?* My mind was still foggy but then reality hit and I finally realized where I was. The Today show was talking about Ground Zero. Of course they were, that was almost all that was on the news the past month. Falling asleep, thinking about it, and having it hit me in the face the minute I woke up gave me concern.

I glanced at my watch, 9:30. Wow, I was tired. I couldn't remember when I had slept so late. I rationalized on why… *I was working the evening shift and needed some downtime when I got back to the hotel. I couldn't just shut my brain down and sleep as the day's events were flashing in front of my eyes and then knowing that I may get to tour the ground zero site had my head spinning! I didn't know if I really wanted to see it!* It got the better of me around two in the morning and I finally succumbed to sleep.

I still had a good five or so hours before I started my evening shift. I was in New York City! Though five hours was not much time, I knew that I had to take advantage of whatever time available I had. I opted to walk around and just get the 'lay of the land'. I could look for a closer subway stop, find a good place to get cheap food, find the nearest grocery. I knew that Red Cross gave the volunteers a stipend, but I didn't want to take advantage of the money that was donated by people from all over the world for this disaster. This money was needed for the victims and their families. I would use this stipend very carefully.

I donned my work clothes, basically dark pants and a t-shirt and stuffed my Red Cross apron in my backpack and headed out the hotel door, knowing I wouldn't be returning that day until after midnight when my shift ended. The day was glorious, a beautiful autumn day, the sun shining brightly with just a hint of crispness to the air. Immediately my mind drifted to September 11th. People must have looked up at that splendid blue sky, similar to what I was doing, and thinking, "wow, this is just a perfect day!"

"It's all set, I have someone that will take over for us while we are touring Ground Zero," Sam said as I approached our First Aid table that afternoon.

"Wow, you didn't waste any time!" I chided. "Are you sure you want to do this?"

"I want to do this for you, Jane, you need to understand this whole operation, feel the impact of it all. I have seen it before but want you to have the complete picture," he insisted.

I stared at him and fidgeted in my seat. I didn't know if I was ready! *Here I go again*, I thought, *it's that flight or fight feeling*. "For being so young, Sam, you are very wise! How did you learn all of that?"

"Oh, my Mom taught me to, um… well, look out for others too, you know?" he laughed.

"Well," I smiled, "your Mom raised you well! When are we heading out?"

"I got it set up that we will hit the Respite Center around 6:00, that's what time Joan is coming over to relieve us," he explained. "We'll have our dinner there and then start walking around Ground Zero."

"We just take off and walk around? Won't we be stopped?" I asked. I was very naïve to all of this but didn't think that we would just be allowed to walk anywhere. Many days later, I found out that we were not supposed to do what we did at that time, and soon many restrictions were put on those that were working there. I decided to just go with the flow.

"We won't know until we try, and I also need to get this cemented in my brain before I head back to L.A. in a couple of days, so I am willing to risk it." He then asked, "Are you getting cold feet?"

"As a matter of fact I am, but what the heck, I'll do this for you, Sam," I acquiesced.

"The Respite Center is a haven, a place for those to go and get away from the pressures and the stress of working on the Pile." Sam explained to me as we were making our short two-block walk to the Respite Center. "There is always hot food around the clock, with <u>great</u> food, just like our place at PS 89, but even better. Most of the Red Cross Disaster Service volunteers are manning this operation here. There's clergy, mental health (or as we jokingly call them, 'the mentals!'), first aid staff (like us), massage therapists and chiropractors are available 24/7. We will have to go upstairs and look at the sleeping rooms, if we can, as that is the most amazing part. It's for those that are working on the pile and need to get a bit of shut-eye. They have these cots set up, like twenty per room and on each cot is a Teddy Bear, or some stuffed animal. These have been coming in, donated, from all over the world for these big guys. They also have a card that some kid wrote to us rescue workers on each pillow, thanking us for our help. Usually there is a piece of candy, a mint, on each cot too. Oh, and there is a TV and computer center, called the Oasis, with big easy chairs. It's on the main floor. There is also a large section, one of the classrooms, where the volunteers are giving out donated supplies to the workers. Things like socks, toiletries, snacks etc. It's like a mini-store, but it is all free. Sometimes they give away new boots and those guys go through so many pairs of boots working on that pile, they really need them and deserve them!"

"This center sounds incredible!" I said. "What was the building used for before this?"

"Oh, it is a university, St. John's University," Sam explained. "I'll let you in on a little rumor I have been hearing, but keep it to yourself, okay? The talk is that we are all probably moving to this Respite Center in the next week or so. Darn, I will miss the move! I guess they want to get this school, PS 89, back up and running again so we are going to be booted out."

"Really? We are going to be moving over to the Respite Center? I wonder if I will still be working First Aid?" I asked.

"No doubt you will be, as there will be a bunch of volunteers heading back home," he said while opening the door of the Respite Center for me. "It's a constant state of fluctuation around here, plus they never have enough medical folks."

We needed to present our ID's when we entered the building as not just anyone could walk into this building; they needed clearance, and have the correct badge that read "Full Access and Ground Zero." It looked as if a small city had popped up in the middle of the university building, much of what Sam had described, but now I was seeing it first hand, with my own eyes. Our first stop was the First Aid station, located near the center of the building on the main floor. It was a circular-shaped room with cubed glass pane windows almost completely surrounding it. It appeared to be a well-designed concept as it was a small room, but so many windows gave it an illusion of being much larger. There were stacks and stacks of first aid supplies intermingled with desks and chairs. Most of the first aid supplies were along the walls and windows, leaving room for the chairs in the center of the room. It was chaotic, but organized in its own way. On the entrance door, someone had placed a laminated 8x11 sheet that stated **First Aid for Heroes. "**How appropriate," I thought to myself.

"So Sam, are you finally working over here? You might as well be as you visit us enough! Hi, you must be new, I'm

Jill," said one of the nurses with one of the most genuine smiles I have ever seen on any human being. I felt at home immediately. Little did I know how close Jill and I would become those many days of volunteering.

"Hi Jill, it's a pleasure to meet you, I'm Jane. Are you in charge here?" I asked.

"Oh heavens, no," Jill said in her sweet lilting voice. "I just follow orders here from Ed and he keeps all of us in line."

"Where are you from? Wisconsin?" I asked.

"Oh, I know we are going to be good friends, Jane. How did you know? Never mind I get it, everyone tells me that my 'accent' gives me away, but most people guess Minnesota!"

"Well, I have relatives in Wisconsin, actually I was born there!" I stated.

"Really? That just makes me smile. I'm missing home, Madison, a lot. I've been here since the beginning."

"So are you heading home next week like Sam is?" I asked.

"No no, I'm extending as I still feel I am needed and can do a bit to help out now and then."

"Fantastic, I'm delighted to hear that you will still be around. Tell me about this first aid area, it looks pretty impressive," I commented.

"The supplies are overwhelming, actually," she started. "They are coming in from all over the country; you know all of the donations. We don't want for anything at all, though our 'patients' jokingly ask us for something stronger than aspirin. They seem to think that we must be a well-stocked pharmacy. Fortunately, we are not, just here to patch them up and give them a few aspirins, and an occasional ear. Most of them come in just to talk."

Jill introduced me to all the nurses working that shift and I developed an instant rapport with everyone. It was a true haven being there, as if the walls protected us all from the harshness of the world. I didn't want to leave, and could see why some many would just come by for a chat, but Sam was standing at the door tapping at his watch.

"We have to get our food now, Jane and then see if we can get that tour, we don't have all night. I wish we did, as you seemed to be really enjoying yourself. I'm glad Jill is here tonight and you got to meet her, she usually works the day shift. You lucked out as she is my very favorite nurse in this whole operation, well… besides you, of course!" he said giving me a wink.

We went through the cafeteria line picking and choosing what we wanted. "Sea bass is on the menu again!" he laughed. "They must have caught a huge amount of sea bass recently as it is a choice almost every single day. See what we have to deal with? It is amazing what they offer here. Let's grab that table over there; those firemen are just getting up."

"Hold on, Sam," smiled a Red Cross worker. "Can you just wait a sec while we wipe down the table and give you a fresh tablecloth?"

"The service here is better than most restaurants, he said, they are on it in a split second." Everyone has their assigned duties and they all take it seriously! Look at how many vultures, er, the Red Cross volunteers, are just waiting to clean things up! Look at that, fresh flowers on every table!"

I looked around the room, and he was right, there were a group of incredibly helpful volunteers just looking for a table to clean. "What's that they are placing next to the salt shakers?" I asked.

"They always have those cards that kids have sent in, like the ones they put on the cots upstairs, for us to read while we are eating. Lots of us read them and take them with us, as a remembrance, but for some it is just too painful and they won't even glance at them," he explained.

I glanced around the room as we sat down; almost every table was filled, mostly with those that were working on the pile. I was surrounded by firefighters, policemen and women, National Guard, FBI, FEMA, OSHA, Red Cross and who knows who else. Their clothes were covered with a fine film of dust and debris, filthy, but no one cared. Their construction hats or firemen's hats were lying next to them on the floor. Some of the guys looked so exhausted that they could barely raise their forks to their mouths and then some were sitting there joking and laughing, and deep into conversations.

"If you continue to stare at everyone, we will never get done with this meal. I'm sorry I am nagging you, but we have lots to do right now. Come on, girl, eat up!"

"I'm losing my appetite Sam. I'm really feeling this to my core. This is just so heartbreaking watching these guys," I sadly replied.

"I'd like to tell you it gets easier, but it doesn't. Let's just talk about our lives outside of this place to get our minds off of it, maybe that will help.

"Again, I have to say this Sam, for someone so young, you are so very mature and as you can probably tell, I am struggling a bit with all of this right now so I really do need your expertise, thanks. Or do I thank your Mom?"

My stomach was in knots, as I knew that I would be checking out the site in just a matter of minutes. Sam was trying so hard to keep my mind off of everything, but I was worried. How would I react?

"Time to get fitted for your respirator," Jason said while getting up from the table.

"Really?" I asked, though I was actually relieved knowing that they wanted to protect us from air that surrounded the Ground Zero site. Little did I realize that we all should have been fitted from the moment we arrived in the Ground Zero area, even where I was working at PS 89. Many of us would come down with respiratory illnesses in the years to follow.

After getting fitted with our masks, we walked out the door to the corner by the Respite Center, next to the Verizon building. A man wearing a Verizon shirt walked over to us. (His building had received major damage.) "Can I offer you a quick tour? It looks like you were ready to take one on your own and I would feel much more comfortable if you would let me show you around," he offered. We quickly agreed and were then given a tour that I will never be able to purge from my mind.

We were surrounded by utter chaos, as if it were a war zone. It was 360 degrees of total devastation. I didn't know if I could ever wrap my brain around what I was being shown. Would this vision always stay with me, somehow I knew it would. It was an experience of such strong raw emotions that I did not know I was capable of feeling. I now understood what soldiers must be feeling in the middle of a battle. No words could be uttered; my throat was tight, as if I had swallowed everyone's grief at that very moment. Thankfully, the respirator would protect me from sharing my blatant feelings with these men. I let the tears freely flow.

Journal entry: October 6th, 2001

This is from my journal and it is very raw, but I wanted to add this to give you a sense of the strong emotions I was feeling.

"I cannot describe it enough to have anyone understand the magnitude of what I saw. Talk about being surreal! I stood on an area that had just been recently cleared just the day before. Ash and silt were everywhere…buildings everywhere destroyed. Large gouges out of buildings where the Trade Towers had collapsed into them. Burned out buildings… gutted. I saw a parking garage that was collapsed with a car totally smashed in it. There was glass and debris everywhere. There were cranes everywhere and workers pulling debris out. Workers coming up to us and thanking us… thanking us! Can you believe it? I, who was doing nothing, was being thanked by those that were doing everything. One worker came up to thank me and said he would feel more comfortable if I was wearing a helmet. He left and came back with one for me. I will keep it forever and remember. I cannot begin to tell you how very overwhelming it was being there, and knowing that it was 2 years ago next month that I stood in that same spot with my friends and looked up at the totally awe inspiring Trade Towers. My mind is having a hard time taking in all that I saw. Smoke… still burning fires, dust, concrete chunks… everything was gray. It was as if I was watching a film in black and white. The sadness of it all just overwhelmed me, knowing that right there so many had lost their lives and there was nothing I could have done to stop it."

Sam and I walked back to our school in utter silence, both of us caught deeply in our own worlds of emotion. What does one say or do after such an experience? How was I to react visibly to anyone about the last 15 minutes of hell that I had just experienced? The weight of the world was lying heavily on me, as I knew it was for Sam. I sensed that he was struggling as much as I was. Silence was our companion.

CHAPTER 9

October 09, 2001 Journal entry

I moved to a new hotel today. My new partner, Connie, from Ontario, Canada, is staying at the Millennium UN. That is where I was originally supposed to stay, but on the first night a group of us Red Crossers arrived and they were full, so we were put up in a Howard Johnson's. I didn't mind terribly, except that the room was dirty and the smoke was really getting to me. Once Connie arrived, we decided it would be much easier to stay at the same hotel so we could go and come from work together. My room is just wonderful with a view to downtown Manhattan, the East River and looking over to Queens and Brooklyn.

Connie and I took the subway to work tonight. It was a new way for us, but we are figuring it out. I feel like I am getting a little more New York-savvy now. Of course, I have a long way to go, but it is fun feeling a bit more comfortable.

When we got up from the subway, we were taken aback by the acrid smell. The workers said it was because the wind was blowing in a different direction. As we passed the site, the smoke was still present, in fact a lot more than I had seen in the previous days. Somehow, going to our first aid station, our little cocoon from all that is going on outside, appears to help. Faces are so familiar at my location and everyone greets me as if we have been friends forever. When the workers come in they come over and shake my hand to say hello... it is a comforting feeling...for us all.

A woman was escorted in tonight to our station, looking for a voucher for an air filter for her apartment. She was finally able to move back in, but all that was in the air was really bothering her. We found out how she could make that happen and invited her to have dinner with us. She was fascinating and was just delighted that we asked her to join us for a warm meal. She is an artist, living in the area, and was given 5 minutes to pack her bags and move out on 9/11. She said that she packed all the wrong stuff, but then how could anyone know what to pack if you were only given a 5-minute warning? She laughed at the things she packed. She said, 'I packed a towel… now why would that be so important?' She stayed for a while in a hotel nearby and then at the Y, then going up to Massachusetts with her daughter, but felt she needed to get back with her people. She tried different areas in NYC, but never seemed to feel she was back with her people… not until she finally was allowed back in her apartment. Her big concern was how she would find her apartment, when her landmarks were gone. She said people that had hardly given her the time of day, in the past, like her mailman and a neighbor, hugged her when she came home. She laughed and said that would only last for a while and then life would probably go back to its more normal state of everyone ignoring each other. She needed to be home because they all had been through a similar experience together. She didn't know how the small businesses there would survive, with lack of access to the area and it might be up to a year before there is any semblance of normal. She feels like she is in Beirut when she walks her street, such a change from being in other areas of New York.

Tonight was my other partner, Sam's, last night. He was anxious for tomorrow, as he only had to out-process at Red Cross and then he and his friends, fellow EMS kids from Southern California, could enjoy the sites of NYC. He was a delight and it was sad to see him leave. Connie and I will do well though, but we just heard that our location would be changing after tomorrow. We are stationed in an International School, and they want to start bringing the kids back. I don't know where we will be headed, but assume it is the Respite Center as Sam mentioned. We are hoping that they will keep the two of us together. Tomorrow we will be getting a tour of Battery Park where some memorials are set up. One of the National Guardsmen has offered to give us a tour, so we are heading into work early for the tour.

While working last night, we realized we did not know where the DMAT was. That is the Disaster Medical Assistance Team, made up of physicians at ground zero. We needed to know where it was in case there was someone that came in and needed more help. We put on our helmets and respirators and off we went... back to Ground Zero. The sites were amazing. It was the six firemen that were heading on duty that I wish I could have taken a picture of, unfortunately cameras were not allowed. They, the firemen, looked so strong and determined and it just almost seemed unreal. Yes, we have all seen the pictures of them on TV, but there they were, appearing larger than life, walking to the site. I will never forget that image. It was Connie's first time seeing the devastation of the area.

The air smells terrible, it permeates through everything. When I wash out my clothes at night, the water is black. I cannot imagine what I am breathing in, but it can't be good. All the workers have scratchy throats and the beginnings of colds.

CHAPTER 10

13 October, 2011- Journal entry

Days are blending together. I have been here over a week now. It is hard to believe. In some respects it seems like I have always been here and how could it be only a week? I woke up from a sound sleep this morning from a nightmare. I dreamed I saw a missile going by my window, where I was working, and was told to get out now. What do I grab?? Then I woke up. We have been hearing rumors of threats in our area, and I am sure that is why I dreamed what I did.

We sent two individuals to the DMAT (Disaster Medical Assistance Team) last night. Therefore, a trip across the Hot Zone (the pile area)to the location. It is good my head is covered with a mask, hard had and protective eye wear, so they don't see me cry. It never gets easier seeing the site, never. They have made a lot of progress in the clean-up, but still… it appears to be never-ending. Behind the shells of the Trade Towers are huge mounds of rubble. The trucks are carting away rubble constantly… there is a long line of trucks waiting to be 'next in line' to take the debris away. I saw 3 or 4 firemen up on top of the rubble, with gloves on, going through it piece by piece. They work constantly, not taking much of a break. They have set up a break area, tents chairs right across from the rubble. Here they are, as we go by, sitting in outdoor chairs, having a coke, with their chairs facing towards the site, not wanting to take their eyes away for very long.. They are my heroes. If you talk to them, they don't feel it like heroes. I heard many work a full shift at their station and then come to the site to volunteer their time.

They, along with all the workers, sometimes come to the Respite 1 Center, where I am working, to have a hot meal, a massage by our massage therapists or to sleep. I have seen them sleeping at their table, while they are eating. They come in to see us at our First Aid Station, occasionally, to get mole skin, cold medication, eye washes. There is so much debris in the air. Sometimes their coats are covered in a dust, looking like snow. Their clothes smell acrid, like the air outside.

CHAPTER 11

I Saw It

Sleeping was sometimes impossible during my work at Ground Zero, as my mind just didn't want to shut down. Images kept playing and I kept seeing in my mind events that led up to and after 9/11. I had many sleepless nights throughout the entire time I volunteered, but it was especially difficult at the beginning. I would feel guilty if I was sleeping, as I saw those firemen and rescue workers at the 'pile' never turning their backs on the site. The site never shut down, it was a 24 hour operation, so how could I feel comfortable sleeping?

I was working the evening shift at PS 89 and I would frequently see the school employee staff, the cafeteria and the janitorial staff. They were very proud of their school and they told me that is why they continued to work, they wanted to make sure that no harm came to 'their place'. The one janitor that I regularly saw, John, caught my attention. He called it *his* school, *his* students. I always enjoyed our brief salutations every evening. He would frequently stop by my table to say hello, or I would see him in the distance and wave.

This particular evening I noticed that John was especially despondent and that concerned me. *Should I talk to him, should I ask how he is doing?* Even though I knew that I was not a Mental Health volunteer, I could see that he was struggling. He kept pushing his broom in the same spot over and over, small little circles. His eyes appeared glazed over, seeming to have no foothold on his true surroundings.

At that point in time, there were no mental health workers volunteering in that building. All the Ground Zero mental health workers were located at the Respite Centers a few blocks from where we were. They were busy taking care of the firemen and rescue workers. I knew that I had to say something to him. I couldn't let him 'slip through the cracks' and become another victim of 9/11.

"Hey John, how are you doing tonight?" I said.

John looked at me as if he was looking right through me. I could see he was just going through the motions at work with such a repetitive nature.

"Hi Jane, I'm not so good tonight," he said, and as I watched, a tear began to form in the corner of his eye.

"I kind of figured that," I said, with worry in my heart. "Do you have a few minutes to sit down at a table and talk?"

He looked around the room and said, "Do you have time to talk to me? Really? I'm the janitor you know, but I really think that would be good. I won't take up much of your time, I promise."

"I DO want to talk to you! You can take all of the time that you need, okay. What's going on John," I said as we sat down. "It looks to me like you are losing some weight."

"So you noticed it too?" he said. "My wife just told me the same thing this afternoon." I noticed a tear sliding down his cheek, then another.

That was my cue, I knew that he needed help and I knew I could do something for him, if only just to listen. I felt I was in the right place at the right time.

"Please tell me what you are thinking about right now, is it something here at work? Is it home? What is it?" I asked.

"I can't eat, I can't sleep, I…I just can't focus on anything. My mind keeps going back to that day and what I heard and saw." He confessed, and then added: "Oh God, it was just so horrible; it is so hard to even talk about it. It's so painful!"

I sat there looking into his sorrowful eyes, waiting for his next words.

"You know, I was in the school when I heard the first plane hit the tower. That is how close we are to the Trade Towers! It shook the building with such force! Everyone wanted to run outside to see what in the world was happening. A group of us stood outside the doors of the front of the school and saw the burning tower. We just stood there staring, not believing. It just didn't seem real." He paused, burying his head in his hands. "And then we saw the other plane."

"Jane," he said. "I saw it hit the building, I SAW IT!! I watched every bit of it. My eyes were so focused on it, I couldn't turn away. It was horrible, I can *still* hear the impact, still see the expressions on everyone's faces that were watching!"

I let him take his time with what he was saying, I didn't want to interrupt. A cold chill was running up my spine. I sensed that he hadn't been able to share this story with many people as it must have been so terribly painful for him to conjure up those memories, to bring it all back to the surface.

I grabbed his hand, "John, I just cannot imagine how horrific that must have been for you."

"I saw them," he said very quietly, as if he was whispering a secret.

"Saw what?" I calmly said letting him lead.

"Oh God, it was the sound first, I just couldn't figure out what it was and I kept hearing it over and over. It wasn't rhythmic, just a sporadic sound," he said barely audible. I had to lean closer to hear what he was about to tell me. Then he locked eyes with me, dead serious and said, "It was the people in the towers on the upper floors, they were jumping out of their burning building! I heard the sounds of them hitting the awnings and the ground before I even knew what it was, and then I looked up and watched. It will never get out of my head, never!"

He began talking with increased speed, as if to clear the memory he had just shared. "We were told that we had to evacuate the school, we had to get our students out of this building, so I went back inside and helped get the kids together so we could get them out safely," he said.

"You know," he paused. "I don't know if I ever will see a lot of these kids again as many of their parents worked in the Trade Towers and died, some just won't come back and some kids will have to move in with their grandparents or aunts and uncles. I was saying goodbye to so many children that day. I know they won't be back at my school and that makes me very sad."

I held his hand tighter. I knew he needed to cry so I let him. His tears affected me too and I quietly sat with him and wept.

He was such a proud man and had experienced more grief in one single day than most people experience in many life times. Words didn't matter at this point, just friendship and support and feeling safe was what he needed.

"Thank you, Jane. I really mean that, it means a lot. You are the *only* one that has asked about me. You are the only one that seems to care. No one wants to talk to a janitor, I feel like I am invisible!" he cried.

"You really need to keep talking about it, John. Can you keep doing that and will you talk to your wife, to a counselor, somebody, anybody? Promise me that you will do that, okay?" I asked.

"I feel like I should do that now, thanks to your getting me to talk. I'm not saying that it won't be hard, but at least I have been able to say the words out loud and not hold them in," he said. Then, he looked around the room, released his grip on my hand, wiped his eyes one last time and stood up. He asked, "Can I please give you a hug? Thank you so much, it means the world to me." We hugged, both of us knowing that we had shared in a story that was so intense. It was hard to let go. As if realizing this, he broke away from our shared embrace, reached for his broom and walked off to the other side of the room.

I just sat there numb for the next several minutes, replaying all that he said to me. I was overwhelmed by his story, but honored that he had felt safe to share his feelings with me. I will never forget that evening so long ago. I think of John often and wonder how things have turned out. I hope he was able to get the help he so desperately needed.

That night as I took the bus back to my hotel room I was quiet the whole way back. I intentionally sat alone because I didn't feel like I could share laughter or conversation with my fellow Red Cross workers. My mind was just spinning thinking about John and his experiences. I felt I had the distinct honor of helping someone who really needed me, and all I did was just listen and give him permission to share. I am a different person from meeting this wonderful proud man.

That night, unlike the many sleepless ones that preceded it, once I laid my head on the pillow, I immediately went to sleep.

CHAPTER 12

Digging Through The Ruin

It had been a long day and some down time away from the site was just what I needed to process the day's events. I eased myself back in the recliner in the room of the Howard Johnson's. They were one of several dozen big motel chains that had come forward in the midst of New York's devastation to donate rooms for volunteers and workers involved with Ground Zero.

Sitting in the cushy recliner, I was thankful for their generosity. I was happy to see that so many big companies were coming forward to help with goods, services, volunteering or donations. Being within the aftermath of some of America's darkest recesses, it helped to be surrounded by so much good in contrast. It helped me balance things in my brain.

After fourteen hours of being on and at the site, I could still hear hisses of the voices from other volunteers and smell the odor of rotting flesh, jet fuel, smoke and debris. It was hard to shake off, harder still to relax enough to sleep.

And yet I desperately needed sleep. My body was totally exhausted but my brain was still vibrant and active, replaying snippets of the day. At least a dozen different suggestions of where and how my time could be better spent over sleeping kept spinning around in my mind.

Somewhere between the wee hours of the morning and the internal introspective chaos my body must have decided it couldn't fight the fatigue any longer and succumbed to sleep. When alas I did open my eyes again the hues of daylight and sunshine splayed through the slits of the window shades.

A part of me felt incensed that the sun was shining. How could it be so pretty outside when there had been such horrific terror? It felt like an affront to me.

I hadn't even gotten to my feet when the phone started to ring. Glancing at the phone on the kitchen counter I noticed the time, it was nearly eight o'clock. Eight o'clock! I never slept *that* long.

"Hello?" I said slowly rubbing the sleep from my eyes. I felt rummy, in need of a good hot shower and fresh coffee.

"Jane, are you coming in soon?" she recognized Phil's voice. Phil was in charge of running the Respite Center, where I had been volunteering. He was a big man that looked a lot like a lumberjack. He had bright red hair and bushy, wild eye brows. In a rugged sort of way he was a handsome man.

I and a number of other Red Cross volunteers had been working closely with him as we all held the title of manger. Phil had an irritating side, in that he could be nit picky and critical but he was also excellent at delegating work duties and keeping things running smoothly. He also had an uncanny way of dealing with people with such positivity, that we didn't realize we were being assigned to more tasks.

Phil showed the utmost respect and admiration for the firemen, policemen and rescue workers that were constants at our Respite Center. Almost all of these individuals would work their regular hours at their own jobs then go over to Ground Zero and work another shift.

I couldn't help but be impressed by their dedication, as well as the uniform way in which many of New York's firemen, police and numerous volunteers worked, so selflessly together trying to make sense of the senseless. Trying to bring order to the chaos and through it all save, rescue and recover the many people that had lost their lives on that fateful day. That day that served as a sad memorial to one of America's most tragic moments.

"Yes, yes. Phil I'm so sorry, I overslept! I never

oversleep!" I exclaimed exasperated. Phil chuckled.

"Be glad you *can* sleep, it took me nearly two weeks before I was finally able to sleep. You never think about what something like that means, until something like this happens," he said, his voice trailing off.

"I'll bet," I answered, thinking about the words. "Anyway, thank you for calling. You were my wake up call! And I'll be there in thirty minutes," I assured.

"Take your time. We'll see you when you get here. Hey thanks, I know it's your day off," he said before hanging up.

I showered in record time that morning and grabbed a fresh pair of scrubs to wear as I managed to sip coffee and work on a eating a bowl of cereal, all at once. I was chastising myself for sleeping, then Phil's words came back to me, and I was thankful that I had slept. I knew I was one of the lucky ones. It made me feel blessed. Thankful.

By the time I arrived at the site, my stomach was already doing flip flops in anticipation of what I might see, might be dealing with today. During my weeks at ground zero I'd seen my fair share of carnage. The images stayed with me like an indelible ink on my heart.

How could people do this to one another? I would never understand it or be able to make sense of it. But then again, could there be any understanding to 9/11? Was it possible to make sense of it beyond it being the atrocity it was?

I quickly made my way through the quiet street, Chambers Street, after leaving the subway station. Chambers is not usually a quiet street but in the wake of 9/11 and so much of the Ground Zero area being cordoned off, it was deathly quiet. I headed towards St. Johns University building, where the Respite Center was located. Smoke and residual vapors hung around the debris and ruined towers like dew on a spring morning. But there was nothing so benign about this scene or about any of it.

An icon of America had been toppled that day just a few weeks before. Had that been the idea all along, to destroy one of America's landmarks? Already rumors were circulating that it had been the work of Al Qaida.

I was not naïve that America had its share of enemies, but until 9/11 I'd never entertained the possibility that their enemies would dare to commit such a heinous act on American soil. Before 9/11 it was always *out there*, some nebulous far-away place. But not anymore. Now the atrocities that I'd only heard about, pertaining to other countries, was now a part of our history, my life, America's reality.

As I started for the temporary quarters of the Red Cross, I again felt a twinge in my gut. What would I see today? What was in store for me? Would there be more survivors or only recovery?

During the last five days, few people had been found, no one had survived. Mostly the firemen were bringing out the fallen heroes, sometimes in only pieces.

For a moment I stopped, I just need to take a deep breath. I'd experienced an inordinate amount of anger and bitterness that was not akin to my personality. But the emotions were there, at the surface, raw and exposed.

Just for being an American I felt violated in a way that prior to this event I'd had no point of reference. I could not even fathom how the victim's families were coping, for their loss was so much more extreme.

In the midst of reflection, I suddenly became aware of a shadow towering over me. I turned to be greeted by Phil, he was smiling, wearing his glasses and his Red Cross vest.

"Well it's about time, Davis," he chuckled as he brushed past. I chuckled too, and felt a slight flush of embarrassment.

"There's a fellow waiting for you in office one, he needs a bit of medical help and didn't want to go to the First Aid Station," he said.

"Thanks!" I said, smiling to myself because I knew that Phil was too far away to have heard.

But in my mind I wondered about his words *a fellow is waiting for you*. What fellow? Who was he? Had he asked for me? And if he had, why?

I opened the door to office one. A wiry, reed-size kind of guy sat quietly, patiently waiting on the fold out chair. The man was wearing a black shirt and black pants that matched his dark auburn hair that was in disarray. From the circles under his eyes, he looked as though he hadn't slept in a week. I smiled, trying to make the stranger feel welcome.

"Hello. I'm Jane…" I started.

"I know who you are," he injected, our eyes met briefly, then he averted my glance.

"Okay," I said softly, sensing I needed to tread lightly around him. "Can you tell me your name?" I asked.

"That's not important!" He said sharply. For another moment our eyes met, but then he nervously looked away. I watched him interlock his fingers, then release them, then lock again.

"All right. So how can I help you? Are you hurt? Do you need some medical care?" I asked, feeling a bit nervous as I sat in the office chair watching him.

For a few moments the man said nothing, just stared at a stuffed FDNY teddy bear on the desk that had been a present that one of the rescuers had given me. I watched him pick it up and stare at it, then return it to the same place on the desk.

Just as I was contemplating calling for help she noticed that big tears had welled up in his eyes. It made me feel

106

conflicted, how to help him. He was clearly in pain but unable to verbalize his feelings.

"Sir, I can't help you if you don't talk to me. I am happy to talk to you about anything you need to but you need to help me out here," I said as calmly as I could make myself sound.

"Steve. My name is Steve," he said. "Don't call me 'sir'" he said.

"Okay, Steve. How can I help you?" I asked again. He looked at me as the tears began to fall.

"Well, I'm not hurt, well maybe a little, just a bit of a cut on my forearm. That's not why I'm here though. Oh God, where do I begin? I saw it. The planes. I heard it. People running everywhere, everything was so out of control. I can see the cloud of debris coming and coming and everyone getting engulfed in it. It's worse than any horror movie I've ever seen! Many good people were lost that day. Why was I spared? There were so many important people…" He cried out, then sunk into a mass of sobs as his big hands covered his face.

The office door opened, Jane saw Phil looking at the man and then at me. I mouthed to him that 'I was okay' so he shut the door silently.

I fought the impulse to hold him and cry with him. I didn't feel okay either. Who could answer such questions?

I tried to convey to him that he was not alone. That 9/11 had left all of America traumatized. But for some of us, like him, that had seen the devastation first hand, it was hard to dismiss, resume their lives as before it had happened.

I wondered how much my words were helping him, impacting him. Were they enough? Would any counseling be enough?

"Steve," I finally said. He looked at me. "I can't tell you that I have an answer for why some of us were spared and others were not, but I can tell you, that we, as the survivors are the ones that have to work together to rebuild America. You need to talk to a professional, Steve, someone that knows much more about dealing with these kinds of issues. I want to thank you for sharing what you said to me, you know, it takes a very strong individual to do what you did."

"Well, I don't feel very strong," he whispered.

"We have a great staff here that is more than willing to listen to you and will also help refer you so you can get the help you so deserve."

His eyes were bloodshot. The weight of his sadness made him look very tired.

"Can I look at your arm?" I asked. He held his arm out to me as if he were giving me a peace offering. It was only a small cut, a bit dirty but didn't look like it needed stitches. "How about you walk with me to the First Aid Station?" I asked. "We will clean that up in no time flat. Then if you want I can introduce you to one of our Mental Health Volunteers." He just nodded, and got up, and followed me out the door.

He turned to me and said, "Thanks Jane, it is the first time I have talked to anyone about it. It's just so hard, so very painful." He grabbed my hand and held it between both of his and just stared into my eyes. Tears were beginning to well up in my eyes and even though I knew it was okay to show emotion, I desperately felt he needed to see some strength.

I broke eye contact with him and patted his hands and said, "No, thank you for feeling comfortable enough to share this with me."

"I was told by several people that you were the one to talk

to. I asked Phil where to find you. I'm so glad you were available."

After he left the First Aid Station I walked back to the now empty office. I was thankful for the silence and solitude. I wondered if Steve was really going to be okay and I wondered if my words really helped. I hoped they did. That had been the goal, the purpose for coming. I picked up my teddy bear and held it tightly in my arms.

CHAPTER 13

Guilt

Days off…. This was, at first, such a guilt feeling, but something everyone told us we needed to do. No one, who was working/volunteering at GZ, wanted to leave, as we felt **we** were there for our mission, there to help, there to serve. How could we enjoy our time while we were there?

Broadway wanted us to come to their shows for only $25 a ticket, restaurants wanted us to come in and dine, and free bus tours were available. New York wanted us to see their glorious city! People opened up their arms to us and truly cared about us. American flags were flying everywhere, there was such a sense of patriotism. It swelled my heart with pride for living in such a great country and having the opportunity to help this incredible and vibrant city. That was the day that I fell in love with New York City.

My first day off of work coincided with my new found friend and co-worker, Connie, and her day off. Connie was also a registered nurse. She was from Ontario, Canada. She and I both felt such guilt for having a day off; we both felt we needed to be at GZ, as we were not there to have fun! We were also very aware that there was so much more that needed to be done. But we were told, YOU NEED A DAY OFF! Our colleagues were right, we did need a day off to get re-charged. For in our hearts we knew it would actually help us accomplish our goal by serving our country better.

Re-charge we did! The first thing we did was go to Central Park and walk just around, take it the sights and sounds of one of New York's premier landmarks. It was a glorious late September day, low humidity, blue skies, a perfect day for a stroll in Central Park.

We both spotted the merry-go-round at the same time, almost as if it had been waiting for us to discover it. Connie looked at me with a mischievous glint in her eyes.

"Jane," she said, all aglow. "Have you ever?"

"No," I confessed.

"Shall we?" she asked with such enthusiasm that I couldn't say no. Ten minutes later there we were with all the children, mounted on our brightly decorated horses, twirling around and laughing like crazy, as if we didn't have a care in the world. It was the beginning of a perfect day!

We took a three hour cruise around Manhattan to see the sites; the cruise line offered discounted tickets to Red Cross Workers. We left from Pier # 83 on the west side of Manhattan and headed south. It was breath- taking, the views were just incredible. Now the Empire State building, mixed with the hundreds of other buildings, towered in the sky line. The roof lines were dotted with the water towers that are so distinctive of the city. As we rounded the corner on the cruise we saw the Statue of Liberty in the distance. There we were, looking at this lady and her symbol of hope and freedom and to our backs was the reason we were there. The gaping space in the midst of all of the buildings in lower Manhattan was an obvious scar. The smoke was still billowing from the site. We were quickly jolted back to reality. We tried not to let it affect our mood as we still had the rest of the day to ourselves and we knew that it would be all too soon until we had to go back to work at Ground Zero but it was right there in our hearts.

We stopped in a local bar to have a drink somewhere around mid afternoon. We were sitting at a booth chatting as if we had been friends our entire lives. It amazed me how friendships formed so quickly there. I felt as if I had known Connie most of my life! A young man stopped by our table and said, "I didn't mean to be listening in, but are you here to help with the aftermath of the World Trade Center?" We told him that we were and he said, "I cannot begin to thank you enough for coming to our city to help. You left your homes and your family and selflessly gave your time to us, you are both such heroes". He ordered drinks for us and thanked us again for our support. These acts of kindness repeatedly happened during the time I was working in New York City. People would give me their seat on the subway and so many just had to stop by to say 'thank you'.

We were totally taken aback by his statement as neither of us felt like heroes. Connie and I discussed that after he left and we both just stared at each other and I said, "Now that is weird! Connie, did you ever think of yourself as a hero?" She said, "Jane, it's as if you were reading my mind, I thought the same thing." I said, "In my mind, the heroes are those working on the pile, not us nurses giving first aid to the rescue workers!" I have never thought of myself as a hero, and it felt odd to hear someone saying that to me/us. I still do not think of myself as a hero to this day. I just was able to take the time from my schedule at home to help those that were the heroes.

The best part of the day was wandering through the streets of Manhattan. For me it was two-fold, one that I was there to see the sites of an amazing city and second, I was getting some much needed exercise! Exercise was one of those things I had completely put out of my head once I arrived in New York for my volunteering. It is amazing that I had totally forgotten about it, when I was such an avid runner and exerciser back at Fort Bragg!

There was so much to see and take in; it was as if I had never been to New York City before. Had it really been only 2 years since I had been to NYC? We, Gary and I, had traveled there in 1999 with our four close friends, two other couples. We were there to celebrate my friend, Fred, and my

100th birthday. Fred was 52 and I was 48, both of us were born on November 4th. I have an amazing picture of the 5 of us (Gary was taking the picture). It was of all of us leaning down to look at the camera and in the background were the two World Trade towers. Gary was lying on the ground pointing the camera up to try to capture the enormity of the towers. I now think about that day and realize that past event cannot be replicated again, it is gone forever.

The fun of the day had been great, and necessary, but now we felt ready, energized, to be returning to our duties, to the call that had brought us to Ground Zero. I had many wonderful days off while in New York City and enjoyed exploring and learning, but none could compare to that first day and the feelings of being re-charged, ready to handle whatever came my way.

CHAPTER 14

Meeting the Light

My first two weeks working/volunteering in New York City were during the evening hours. I would arrive at the Respite Center at 4:00 in the afternoon and then work until midnight. I remember the day, Friday, the 19th of October. I had just gotten out of the shower and I had the television on tuned to my favorite show *The Guiding Light*. Ever since we lived in Germany, 1987-1992, I began watching *The Guiding Light* soap. Really there was only one choice of television station back then, so whatever was on we watched. That is how I became an enthusiastic viewer and had been pretty addicted ever since.

A light bulb went off in my head; this was the city where the show was filmed! Wow, what an opportunity! On a whim I looked up the phone number for the show's studio and gave them a call. If it was at all possible, I wanted a tour and hopefully to even get an opportunity to meet some of my favorite stars.

"Hello," I said.

"I am a volunteer working at Ground Zero," I continued, "And I am an avid fan of the Guiding Light! So I just had to call to find out if you offer tours of the set?"

"I am sorry to tell you, we are not giving tours anymore, due to September 11th," the man at the other end of the phone said.

"You know that they are having their big fan club event this weekend, 'The Gathering', he said. "I am sure the person in charge of the event, Debbie, would love to hear from you, maybe she can get you some tickets."

He gave me Debbie's phone number and I thanked him. I put down the phone and thought, Jane *what the heck are you thinking? Why are you doing this? You should be focusing only on your work at Ground Zero! This is so frivolous!*

Work had been particularly stressful lately. People, both the workers and volunteers, were irritable, seeing no end in sight. I knew that I too needed a break as their irritability was wearing off on me. I was catching the irritability myself. I had the next day off from work, and didn't have to be back until Sunday late afternoon. I knew how important it would be for me to clear my head, and focus on something totally different, if even for such a short time. For that reason I ignored my negative thoughts and made the phone call to Debbie.

"Hi, my name is Jane Davis and I am a Red Cross volunteer nurse working at Ground Zero," I began. "I was given your number by Jason, at the studio and he told me that there is supposed to be a Guiding Light fan club event this weekend," I paused.

"Oh my goodness," Debbie gushed. "You're my hero!"

"Well, I don't know about that," I stammered taken aback. I certainly didn't think of myself as a "hero."

"It would be an honor and a privilege for all of us if you could meet us tomorrow at the bowling alley at the Port Authority. They are having an event there, where the fans get to meet the stars," she said. "Can you come, or do you have to work?"

"Tomorrow happens to be my day off," I exclaimed feeling elated. "I would love to come by."

"Well here is what you need to do," Debbie started. "Go to the floor where the bowling alley is. You will see a long line of people, fans, waiting to go in. You should go past all of them and go to the door and tell the person there that you are to come in and see me. She will have your name. Oh, Jane this is just so exciting, I am just thrilled that you can come!"

I went to work that evening recharged and with a clearer

mind. I had something fun to look forward to, something that would allow my spirit to soar free for a while and I was in dire need. There's only so much human tragedy one person can handle. This was just what I needed!

That night seemed to be a better one, maybe it was just my improved attitude as I had a better outlook, but it seemed more than that. I noticed that even the rescue workers were more talkative, as if there was an unspoken code word to keep their emotions lighter. Some of them were even telling jokes. It was clear that we all needed to smile every now and then. I was elated to see the change, small as it was it was still a change.

As if kismet were smiling on me, there were fewer injuries that evening and I didn't have to take any ill or wounded workers across the pile to see one of the doctors (a welcomed reprieve). Those that came in that evening needed only Band-Aids for small cuts or mole skin for sore feet. It was an easy night, and most just wanted to come in to 'talk to their favorite nurses.'

I kept my bowling event to myself. I was unsure why, was it because it was mine and I didn't want to share it or was it because people would think I was silly? Why did I care? But apparently I did, at least on some level. But nothing was going to slow me down.

I left work smiling knowing that I had Saturday off and didn't have to return until Sunday in the later afternoon. I had a very difficult time trying to fall asleep with so many thoughts floating around in my brain. *Should I be doing this? What should I wear? Why do I deserve a day off?* Eventually the thoughts quieted and around 2:00 a.m. I finally fell asleep.

After about 5 hours of sleep I woke up quite refreshed and got ready for my *fun* day. I took the subway to the Port

Authority and found my way to the bowling alley. For some reason I was just amazed that there was a bowling alley in that building!

Just as Debbie said, there was a long line of women at the door of the bowling alley. I walked by all of them, not daring to look at them as I was sure that they were all staring at me wondering who the Princess was going to the front of the line.

I knocked on the door and waited. When the door opened, the woman who answered had a smile on her face. When I told her who I was the woman at the door burst into a huge smile and said, "Come on in Jane, Debbie is waiting for you over there!"

I walked into the bowling alley and saw Debbie was busy working out the last minute arrangements for the big event. Immediately I went up to her and told her who I was. Just then, she stopped doing what she was doing and threw her arms around me very excitedly. "Everyone, this is Jane, the volunteer I was telling you about, our very own hero!"

Debbie said that the event would be starting in about an hour and said that I could go wait in the lounge. I quizzically looked at her and said, "sure!" Debbie looked at me and smiled mischievously and said, "Jane, all of the soap stars are in there now, meeting with each other and doing interviews with the soap magazines. Go have fun!"

She saw my face and just laughed. "Really Jane, they are great people and you won't feel intimidated at all, in fact I think that they will be intimidated of you!"

"I really doubt that!" I said.

"I'll tell you what, I will go in with you and introduce you to a few people," Debbie said. Well that was a relief! I had been sweating it, how to approach all these stars, but Debbie's easy going charm had helped me to relax.

I walked in the door of the lounge and there were all the celebrities that I knew so well from watching the show. I worked hard to keep my composure and not act like a love struck fan, which I was and felt in my heart but I was determined that they didn't need to know that!

Debbie did as promised and began introducing me to Michael O'Leary, who played the role of Rick Bauer and Crystal Chappell who played the role of Olivia Spencer. Michael's character was such a nice guy, one that would never do anything wrong, and that is how he appeared in real life. Crystal on the other hand held the role of villain, and I was unsure what to expect! Nothing could have been further from the truth; she was so friendly and outgoing. Such a petite woman dressed so casually and immediately made me feel relaxed. I did not feel intimidated at all! I was totally amazed how relaxed both were and how they treated me as if *I* was someone special… *me*!!

"So you are really working at Ground Zero?" Crystal exclaimed. "What is it like? How did you decide to volunteer and how does one go about volunteering there?" These were the common questions throughout the day from everyone that I talked to. It continued to astound me how interested they were in hearing about an ordinary person like me. Michael and Crystal began introducing me to the other soap opera actors so Debbie was able to go back to her work.

For the next hour I was introduced to everyone that came for the event. I spent a good amount of time talking to Robert Newman who played the role of Josh Lewis on the show. As luck would have it when I went up to the bar to order something to drink, Grant Aleksander, who played the role of Phillip Spaulding sat next to me and had a drink with me. I was delighted to learn he was just a regular kind of guy who like his colleagues liked hearing about my work at

Ground Zero.

It felt unnatural for me to be treated like the celebrity amongst all these stars, and yet I was. In fact, some of the soap opera magazine writers were there and they interviewed me. Unfortunately those interviews never made it in to the magazines, but it was still quite an honor to be interviewed.

At the end of the hour, they got everyone together for a group picture. I was standing on the side lines watching when one of the cast members saw me and said, "We need Jane in this picture too!" So I obliged and posed with them.

I found myself feeling sad that the hour was up; it had gone by so quickly. But I had such a great time with memories that would last me a life time. So when Debbie came up to me and asked about the bowling, I'd nearly forgotten why I had come.

"What size bowling shoes do you need?" she said again. I had to pause. It was all so incredulous!

"Size 6 ½" I told her. Then she dropped the bomb.

"Who do you want to bowl with?" she asked.

"Are you kidding me?" I asked. She said that she was absolutely serious and I could pick *anyone* that I wanted.

"Can I bowl with Robert Newman?" I asked sure she'd say no. But to my surprise
and delight she didn't hesitate for a second.

"Perfect, I will put you with him and a few of the other fans," she simply said. I was speechless. What could I say to *that*?

Well, first of all, I love to bowl! I have been on leagues for a good portion of my life. Not only was I going to get to do something I thoroughly enjoyed but also bowl with my favorite soap stars! I just kept thinking that someone needed to "Pinch me." This couldn't really be true, could it?

It was fun; no it was *more than fun*! It was fabulous.
Everyone was laughing and snapping pictures and just
enjoying life. I almost forgot for a few minutes why I was in
New York City. I just kept thinking how often does someone
get to do this kind of thing?

Robert spent a good amount of time talking to me about
my work at Ground Zero and he was just totally amazed.
He asked me many questions including the one that nearly
every one asked me, "How can I help, how can I volunteer?"
It was a familiar theme. It made me realize that most
Americans really did want to help.

At the end of bowling, Robert pulled me aside. "Jane,
several from our cast are doing a play reading in town
tonight, my wife and I will be reading also. Can you by
any chance come and watch? We will be reading The Glass
Menagerie".

I couldn't believe I was hearing him correctly, (he
was asking me to come to this event and I was amazed)
immediately I said, "This is just perfect, I am off this evening
and don't have to be back to work at Ground Zero until
tomorrow evening!"

"Really?" he was pleased. "The big luncheon is tomorrow
afternoon, this is where all of us meet the fans and it is such a
good time, with videos, singing and much more. Why don't
you check with Debbie to see if they can get you into the
event?" My brain was reeling.

"That is such a generous offer." I finally stuttered, "I
will go and talk to Debbie now and see what she says about
tomorrow and thanks for the offer tonight, I am really looking
forward to it!" I walked over to Debbie. She'd been working
on some paperwork but looked up when I came over.

"Thanks so much for making this happen for me, Debbie;
I just had an absolute blast!   Robert has asked me to go to

his play reading tonight, which I will if that is okay! He also asked me if I was going to the luncheon tomorrow. I didn't even know about it!" Debbie pulled me aside and gave me a hug.

"Jane, you deserve some special treatment, after all that you are doing at Ground Zero! I love that you don't know about the luncheon, the Gathering. You are a fan but not obsessed about it! Do you have tomorrow off and would you be able to attend the luncheon?" she asked. I had to think, I knew I had to be there by three.

"Well, I work later in the afternoon, so I could come for some of it," I told her.

"Fantastic! Of course the event has been sold out for weeks now, but let me see what I can do. Why don't you show up at the Roosevelt Hotel tomorrow morning around 11:00 and come talk to me. I will get you in. The event will be held in their ballroom, but come to the sign in desk and talk to me," Debbie instructed.

I went back to my hotel room elated! Could this really be happening? Did I really get to meet everyone? Not only had I had an unbelievable event that night and then again in the morning... but with more to come... truly this really was a Guiding Light weekend!

That evening, I took the subway to the Helen Hayes Performing Arts Center and was guided to the room where the play was to take place. I walked up to the table to sign in and pay but much to my chagrin the woman behind the counter said to me, "Oh, this has already been paid for by Robert Newman!" I was floored! *He paid for me to come to this event?* I was beyond thrilled! Did he have any idea how deeply his kindness affected me?

I thoroughly enjoyed the performance of the Glass Menagerie. Afterwards I chatted with Robert and thanked him for being so gracious. I went home feeling totally delighted. This was just what I had needed that weekend! I needed to be taken away, if even for a short period of time, from Ground Zero. From the ugliness, bleakness of that tragedy, that day that forever blemished our virgin country. That before 9/11 had been a country unfettered by terrorism. But alas, not anymore, we now all lived in a different world.

The next morning I awoke to check the city map. I needed to find out where Roosevelt Hotel was located and found out that it was on 45th Street. I planned my route to there on the subway and then to return to Ground Zero afterwards on the subway. It didn't seem too difficult and I was getting to feel pretty comfortable at navigating my way around the city.

I arrived at the beautiful Roosevelt Hotel at noon and followed the crowds so I knew where to go. As before, Debbie was there to greet me. I had my money in hand to pay for the luncheon and sit with all of the fans. But again I was redirected.

"Oh no, that won't do!" Debbie exclaimed. "I have already set it up that you will be going to the Green Room and have lunch with the cast members."

"Are you kidding me?" I said incredulously.

"Absolutely," she said. "I have to treat my very own hero especially, don't I?" Debbie gushed.

The star treatment was beginning to overwhelm me. I was not ungrateful, contrarily I was *very* grateful, but I wasn't accustomed to being treated with such praise. It just didn't feel like me.

I walked into the Green Room, a little apprehensive, but tried my best to look like that was where I was supposed to be. I saw one of the new cast members, Jim Davidson, sitting at a table by himself reading a Soap Opera magazine. His role on the show was as Alonzo Baptiste, the brother of

Prince Richard of San Cristobol.

It puzzled me to see him alone so I asked Jim why he was reading the magazine by himself.

"Well I am pretty new to the show and I see all of these cast members here and I don't know who many of them are!" was all he said. But that was enough. Immediately I tried to help him out the best I could by pointing out the different cast members and explaining who they were.

"Look," I pointed. "There's Mary Stuart, she plays the role of Aunt Meta Bauer." Little did I realize that in a short three months Mary would pass away.

"Do you know who that is?" I said pointing to Billy Kay who played the role of Shane Lewis. "He's is Josh's son."

Then I excused myself to get some food. I was taken aback by the banquet, there was quite a spread of food there! It was overflowing with anything anyone would want, all assortments of meats and cheeses, salmon and shrimp. Every salad imaginable seemed to be there and many I had never seen before. I was thinking to myself, *if this is how they eat, how do they stay in such great shape?* My stomach was feeling like butterflies had moved in, so I just made myself a small plate. I took my food and then went back and sat down with Jim. As everyone else was starting to sit down my table was beginning to fill up.

Everyone seemed so happy to see me again and the conversations just flowed so smoothly. I was so thrilled to have two of my favorite characters sitting at the table with me. They were Elizabeth Kiefer, who played the role of Blake and Jerry verDorn, who played the role of Ross, her husband. They both were so down to earth that it made me feel relaxed. And surprisingly they also were so impressed with the work I was doing in their city. I was just blown away with everyone being impressed with me! Because to

127

me, it was not some heroic duty, it was a necessity. I had to help, it was in my blood. I always had to reach out.

After lunch, it was time to go in and meet the fans, who had already had their lunch in the ballroom. They brought me out in the ballroom and gave me a seat very close to the front, so I would have a great view of the performance that was about to take place. They had thought of everything!

The show was just fantastic, with singing and videos and great stories. It lasted for a long time and I was beginning to get nervous that I wouldn't see it all, as I had to head into work soon. If fact when I looked at my watch, I saw I only had half an hour left. But I was in luck, the show was winding down and I saw Debbie going on stage with a large check.

"Before I tell you how much money we are donating to the 9/11 fund I want to tell you about the hero I met the other day and she is here with us today," Debbie said. "Her name is Jane Davis and she is a Registered Nurse from Fort Bragg, North Carolina and she is here to volunteer her service and time at Ground Zero. Jane, will you please stand up!?"

I stood up immediately on shaky legs. I could feel my heartbeat in my throat. Just then Ricky Paul Golden, who played the role of Gus, stood up and began clapping. Then the entire cast of *Guiding Light* stood up and clapped and then the entire audience stood up! They were all smiling and clapping at me! I mouthed the words *Thank You*. I was embarrassed and thrilled all rolled into one.

Finally the event was over. But as I got up and walked back into the Green Room I knew it was a memory that would stay with me throughout my life. I got my backpack so I could leave and get on the subway. It was time to get back to work.

Almost immediately some of cast members came over

and started giving me their phone numbers, they asked me to get in touch with them so that they could help. Ricky came up to me as well and introduced me to his girlfriend then he thanked me again. But I kept thinking I should be thanking them, but yet it was they who were doing the gratuities.

Everyone was busy talking to each other and hugging each other and I took it as my cue to sneak out the door and head to the subway. I threw the backpack over my shoulder and quickly headed for the exit.

However I didn't get far because I needed to stop at the restroom to change my clothes for work. It was there that I over heard some of the luncheon fans whispering, *there she is, that's the woman volunteering at Ground Zero!* A few women came over and thanked me. I could sense that they really wanted to talk, but as I glanced at my watch I realized I would really have to hurry just to make it on time. So I thanked them and scurried out the door towards the subway.

It turned out to be a very busy and stressful night. My memories of the day seemed far away. I never told any of those I worked with at Ground Zero about my weekend event. I guess there are some things we all need to keep just for ourselves.

The next day, I sat down and wrote them a letter explaining how greatly I appreciated their kindness. It was then that I explained how they could help. (I had first contacted the headquarters of the American Red Cross and received all of the information). I faxed it on to the CBS station. I decided not to telephone any of them and keep it as professional as I could. That way it would truly be up to each person as to what they did or didn't do.

It was days after before I had much of a chance to reminisce about my experience and even more days before I shared it with friends and family at home. There never seemed to be an appropriate time to bring it up at work. I was sure that people at work wouldn't understand and think of my weekend as frivolous.

But on a personal level I will never forget the caring and compassion that everyone from the Guiding Light cast showed. It warmed my heart and soul. For me it was so important to see the people that I had watched on television for years, being so normal and caring. It gave me a renewed hope for life itself.

CHAPTER 15

Nowhere

My first three weeks at Ground Zero had flown by and I was told it was time to return home. It just didn't seem right that with so much work needing to be done that I was told it was time, time to go back to my life before, when I was not ready. My family was eager to see me again, as within the next few days I would be celebrating a milestone birthday. *Who cares*, I thought, I just wanted to stay in New York City. I also needed to return home as we had a mini-vacation planned with Gary and a few of my friends, to take a cruise called the Cruise to Nowhere.

"Jill, I can't leave now!" I wailed. I need to come back as I am not ready to put closure on this!"

"Why don't you chat with Jean and see if there is a possibility you can come back here to the Respite Center?" Jill suggested.

"What sort of chances do I have to get that to happen?" I asked.

"Well, it never hurts to ask," Jill stated. "Plus there is a big volunteer group changing out to include our First Aid Supervisor, Frank. We will need a replacement for him."

"I assumed that you would be taking that role over," I said.

"Oh, no, not me! I'm a worker bee, and am not one that wants to do a supervisor role, but Jane, this is right up your alley!" She exclaimed, getting more animated as she talked in that Wisconsin lilt. "I'll talk to Frank about it and have him mention it to Jean. I'll mention it to her also. I think you are a shoe-in for taking the supervisor's role and it makes sense to have someone do it that has been here and understands the whole process."

I mulled it over in my mind. I knew that I could handle it, though it would be a big responsibility. "I would appreciate if you would help with that Jill. I HAVE to come back here; I'm just not ready to finish this yet!"

An hour later I decided that I would give Jean a call and see how persuasive I could be to encourage her to put a good word in for me.

"Jane, it is highly unlikely if you come back, you will return to the same location. That usually doesn't happen," Jean said into the phone. "I will see what I can do as I know this is important to you. I've already talked to Jill and Frank and they have been VERY persuasive though I don't want you to get your hopes up. I'll try to push it, but the final decision is out of my hands. Go home as I know you have all sorts of things going on, recharge and we will go from there."

"Jean, please don't forget about me once I go home! I'm not ready to stay away and if it wasn't for the fact that this stupid cruise was already planned, I'd be staying here. How often can I call to see if it can be arranged?"

"I'll work on it Jane! I promise. My you are one persistent woman! Give me a call in a week and I will have an idea by then. Oh, I know you and I can tell by the look on your face that there is no way you will hold off for a week!" she laughed.

"Will you be here when I get back?" I asked.

"Absolutely I will be. I don't have any commitments back home so they are stuck with me. I'm sure a few of the nurses here would wish that I would head back, they think I'm a tough old bird," she chided.

"Well," I said. "I surely don't feel that way about you; you have always been fair to me!"

"I like to think I am, fair that is. But Jane, you and I have a special bond." She paused.

"You know I really do value our working relationship Jean. I love to get your phone calls, you always brighten my day!"

"Or darken someone else's doorstep!" she teased.

I loved my relationship with Jean over the past three weeks and couldn't imagine why others wouldn't feel the same way. She treated me fairly and kindly and as an adult who could make the correct decisions. I guess, kind of like a Mom would do, something that I wish my own mother would have done for me.

Arriving home

Simple as it sounds, I did NOT want to be home. I loved my family and they all knew it, but I know that they all sensed my heart was still back in New York City. The only way to survive with family and friends was to put on an act, hold my head high, and move into their reality. My mind kept focusing on Ground Zero.

The phone was constantly ringing, friends kept stopping by. It was as if I had gone to war and they were welcoming back their soldier. I worked on being gracious and kind and put on that happy face they all wanted to see. Everyone wanted to hear my story. How does one tell the story of my experience over and over to hold that same passion that I was feeling inside? I found myself pulling back, *how could they understand*?

Two days later we traveled down to Norfolk, VA to board the cruise ship to take us nowhere. Truly, it was called the *Cruise to Nowhere*. We would be gone for three days; two nights out to sea, turn around and return to port. My friends and I had booked this trip several months before September 11th had darkened our doorsteps. "Jane, you can do this and have a good time. You are allowed to, you know?" Gary said. "Forget things for a few days, it will be good for you! It will be good for me, I'm just so glad that you are back at

136

home, I have really missed you!"

If one wants a culture shock, it would be to go on a cruise in the middle of two stints at Ground Zero! I was overwhelmed, how dare these people celebrate and have fun and only a mere 350 miles away is our country's own war zone? It was extremely difficult for me to take the frivolity all in, the incongruence overwhelmed me. I emphatically knew that I must succumb to these events and embrace them for what they were. Who knew, maybe this was my oasis, doesn't everyone deserve a break from life's cruelties?

Okay Jane, just get the deer-caught-in-the-headlights look off your face, relax and work on enjoying yourself! I thought to myself. I knew I could do it if I tried hard enough. *Have a drink, visit with your dear friends and husband because, as you know, they so want you to have a good time!* My pep talk to myself seemed to work and I was able to actually enjoy the time, or at least make them all believe that I was part of the living.

Surprises

I had promised myself I would not call Jean while I was on my cruise. Gary deserved a few days of vacation too, as his schedule after 9/11 had been insurmountable. I had to make that phone call though; I had to find out if any progress had been made toward my return to Ground Zero. We had barely parked the car out front of our house at Fort Bragg when I dashed up to my room to grab Jean's phone number. I nervously dialed the number.

"Jean, its Jane, has any progress been made on my return?" I asked out of breath.

"Didn't I tell you to wait a week? I told you Jane, but I knew you couldn't do it! How are you? How was your cruise?" she quipped.

I could hear the smile in her voice which made me relax. I settled into a chair and grinned. "Jean, you know me too well. We had a blast! I just arrived back home, and made a beeline to the phone to call you."

"I figured I would hear from you sometime today. Well I have some news for you that I think you will like. You need to book your flight back to the city next Tuesday. Will that work for you?" She asked.

"Absolutely it will work, but you are not telling me something, where will I be working?" I pleaded.

"My, oh my, are you impatient! I did my magic and by the way, You Owe me Girl! You are coming back to the Respite Center to be the supervisor of the First Aid area."

Gary peered in the doorway as I let out a little yelp and mouthed the words, "you okay?" I nodded my head, beaming from ear to ear.

"I do want you to know that this is highly unusual as you don't have the experience on disasters. This is your first one, right?" she asked. "Usually we take a more seasoned disaster volunteer, but your glowing recommendations from the Respite Center paid off."

"Well technically this one will be my second disaster, since I took some time off in-between, right?" I laughed.

"I guess you are right, you are more seasoned than I thought," she chuckled. "With your wonderful background as a nurse, volunteer and leader, your experience speaks for itself. Unfortunately Jane, I don't have time to chat. I have a line of new recruits waiting to steal your position. So hurry back or I will fill it! I look forward to seeing you on Tuesday and by the way, Happy Birthday!"

"Thanks for everything Jean and thanks for putting a good word in for me. I'll see you in a few more days." I beamed.

"Love you honey," she exclaimed.

"Love you too."

"So, you're looking awfully happy! By the sound of the conversation, I guess you are leaving me again," Gary teased.

"Not only going back to New York, but I will be the First Aid supervisor at the Respite Center! I can't believe it! I leave on Tuesday," I gushed.

"Well it is well deserved! I'm happy for you, but I will miss you. It has been great having you back for a bit. I'm being selfish, I know," he stated, "but I like having you around. I know that your mind is much occupied with all of this and your heart is really back there. I see it, but don't forget about us here, okay?"

"It won't be forever. I will talk to you every day and keep you updated," I promised.

"You know, your birthday is in two days. I'm glad you will be here for that. It's a big one!" he laughed.

"Oh, don't remind me! Actually I had been dreading this birthday, but now after all I have seen and been part of, I just feel pretty darn lucky to be alive," I said.

"I am the one that feels pretty lucky; I have you in my life!"

"Don't get sentimental on me, okay? So what are we doing for my birthday?" I asked. "I know that Melissa and Mark are coming down to see me. Dinner or what? Please, no parties. I'm just not up for that."

"They will be in tomorrow and I thought we would have dinner somewhere, maybe somewhere close by," he suggested. Little did I know but this had all been planned weeks in advance!

"Sounds fine to me!" I said squeezing his hand.

My sister and Mark arrived the next day eager to share in my birthday celebrations. It was great as always to see them and we all seemed to just pick up on life, right where we left off. Mark and Gary had become great friends which made it delightful when the four of us got together.

"Janie you are finally going to be 50!" Melissa exclaimed. "It's about time, now you are part of the club!"

"Oh, please, don't remind me," I joked. "You do know, Melissa, that I will never be as old as you!"

"Haha, so funny Janie!" she laughed.

I have truly loved my sister as we have shared in so many of life's critical moments together and each one just strengthened our bond. We were there for each other when we heard the news of our little brother, Scott's drowning. We were a phone call away when our father died, I was in Germany and she was with him for his final breath. We were there for each other at our weddings and divorces. These were such defining moments and I began thinking to myself how lucky it was for me to have her in my life, especially as an adult. As a child, not so much though. She is three and a half years my senior and when we were kids, I was her little pesky sister who was very jealous of the relationship she shared with our mother. I cherish our time now.

"Let's toast to my baby sister and the BIG five-oh," she said holding up her Budweiser. We all laughed and toasted. I had a feeling there were going to be many toasts the next couple of days.

We arrived at the restaurant shortly after 5:00 pm and I heard a deep voice say, "Well look at that, my baby sister is fifty!"

"I recognize that voice!" I squealed and ran over and gave my brother Martin a big hug. He and his wife, BL, were both standing there beaming. "When did you get in from Kentucky? I had no idea that you would be here!"

"We thought you would like a little surprise, plus this is

a big weekend for you! We are so proud of you and all that you are accomplishing little sis! We arrived about an hour ago, just time enough to get settled in the hotel. Gary has been a busy guy planning this weekend," he winked.

"The big day isn't until tomorrow, so I am still 49 and am holding onto it as long as I can possibly do so," I informed everyone.

Catching up with family is so wonderful and we must have stayed at the restaurant at least two hours. There was never a lull in our conversations. Finally Gary glanced at his watch said, "Let's go back, Diane wants us to stop by, she made a cake."

To my surprise, we drove up to the house and found a large group of friends and family hiding behind the trees, jumping out and wishing me a Happy Birthday. I had no idea, I was dumbfounded! Tears were streaming down my face, tears of joy! Not only did my brother, sister and siblings come, so did my son Ian and daughter, Elizabeth, her husband James and our grandson JT. The only one missing was my Mom, but it was rare to get her to go anywhere any more. It seemed as if all of Fort Bragg was there that evening and it was a great way to catch up with everyone.

"Did we surprise you?" Diane asked me when I walked into her kitchen. "We have been planning this for weeks you know. I was so afraid that you wouldn't come back from New York and then we would have had to have the party without you!" she laughed!

"What a shock, I had no idea at all. I told Gary I didn't want a party, but secretly," I whispered in her ear, "I am thrilled! But don't tell Gary!"

"I think he knows Jane," she said giving me a hug.

"Thanks Diane for putting this together. It really took a lot of work and planning, you are the best!"

"For you, my friend, anything!" she laughed.

Return

The return flight was non-eventful, fortunately this time they booked me from Fayetteville, NC! I immediately returned to my usual duties at the Respite Center, this time working the day shift, from 8-4. I was delighted with the daylight hours but was told that by having the role of supervisor, I was expected to overlap with each of the other shifts. I would be in charge of all of the nurses at the Respite Center and would need to evaluate them. How could I evaluate if I wasn't working with them?

I assumed my second trip back to volunteer would be easier, as I had already experienced such raw emotions the first time around. Unfortunately that was not the case. Jean informed me that I would need to live closer to the Respite Center. The rationale was if there would be an issue at the First Aid room, I could arrive to help in a moment's notice. I was told I would be moving to Battery Park City in an apartment just opposite of the Ground Zero complex. The location was excellent and the living quarters were ideal. I had a kitchen, living room, bath and bedroom. The person that was living in the apartment had never returned after 9/11; therefore Red Cross was able to acquire it. I must admit, my mind kept wondering, where was the owner of this apartment? I had many sleepless nights while living there and the first week I could not even sleep in the bedroom. I kept having visions that the owner was one of the unfortunate ones that did not make it out of the Trade Center. My major concern was that the living room window had a view of the Trade Towers, which meant my view was of the Pile. At that time it was a 24 hour operation, therefore the whole area was lit up as if it were day time. The curtains remained closed. I seemed to never be able to turn off the sights and smells of Ground Zero. Living so close to work, had its price.

My walk to the apartment, from the Respite Center, was a beautiful one, the Hudson River on my right, and off in the distance I could see the Statue of Liberty. I would frequently pause just to take in this view. There she was standing strong, Lady Liberty, never wavering, and welcoming those from faraway lands. In front of me was the hope of our nation's future, behind me was utter devastation.

As my route home continued I would walk by Pump House Park. Traveling down Liberty Street, the park was to my left. Being outside the perimeter of Ground Zero, the public had access and could visit this location and pay their homage. Everyone, it seemed, wanted to leave some sort of memento, a memorial to those lives that were immediately silenced on 9/11. Many left stuffed animals, mostly teddy bears hence the name that we called the site; the Teddy Bear Wall. It was very emotional for me to halt my travels and observe this memorial every day as I walked my route. *Keep walking Jane, just get past it and move on*, I would chant to myself.

Rounding the corner on Liberty I walked past several stores, grocery stores, banks, restaurants… everything that a typical neighborhood in Lower Manhattan would have. The only difference, they remained closed and had not reopened since 9/11. Peering in the grocery windows I could see items in their bags still left on the counters, debris covering the floors. The plants in the windows of these establishments tore at my heart strings. They were left behind, neglected and dying as no one was allowed to come back in to care for them. Daily they would wilt at bit more, until there was nothing left of them but brown stalks. The most heartbreaking was looking at the Winter Garden on Vesey

Street. This distinctive building received a major hit from the fallen towers, with almost every single pane of glass destroyed. Two thousand panes had to be reconstructed. The forty foot *Washingtonia Robusta* palm trees slowly perished. I always visit the Winter Garden, when I return to Lower Manhattan and sit on the renovated marble steps, looking out at the glorious atrium and the sixteen new palm trees and remember.

The sights, sounds and smells of Ground Zero will always be there in my mind and I can drum them up at a moment's notice. The overwhelming distraught feeling has been replaced by my current life. I have moved on, but I will not forget. I always say that when something tragic happens to an individual it is as if it were an open wound, weeping and raw, just touching it may make it bleed. Over time this wound forms a scab, but any little hurt or remembrance can make it ooze. Eventually, over a longer period of time, a scar forms. We will always see it as it has become part of us, and we will always remember, but we can move on.

CHAPTER 16

Stalked!

I was stressed, and so busy that I had little free time. Schedules needed to be made; evaluations had to be written for each individual, not to mention the plethora of meetings that I was now required to attend. The Respite Center was a large operation that needed to work like a well oiled machine. The Respite Center supervisor, Phil, was not computer literate and I would always know he needed some help when he walked in the First Aid Station. It was something about the look on his face, pathetic I guess, hoping I would run upstairs and set up a spreadsheet for him! I did so willingly, as I just loved being part of the organization.

My medical team was extraordinary and it made my job so easy. They were so eager to help, some giving weeks and weeks of their time, like Jill, and others giving a few 8 hour shifts, the local volunteers. Any amount of time was helpful. Most of my volunteers were nurses or EMT's, but Dan was an Orthopedic Surgeon and he loved to give me grief about my being his supervisor! I relished it. Dan, Jan and Darlene had a two week assignment with me. Dan was from Colorado, Jan from California and Darlene from Massachusetts. We all were developing a strong bond with each other. The Triple J's formed in mid-November, Jill, Jan and Jane. We were inseparable! We worked together all day, had dinner and drinks at night and shared in each other's lives. It was amazing that in such a short period of time our friendships grew deep. Darlene and Dan were a very big part of our little group; unfortunately, they didn't have a "J" in their name! I could count on them for anything. I knew that they had my back and I had theirs.

A new group of local volunteers had arrived at the Respite Center. It was a revolving door trying to keep up with all of the new medical folks that wanted to help. They had already in-processed at headquarters and were bused to our Respite Center eager to get to work.

Our newest local recruit was Jared. He was different than the rest, and I just couldn't pinpoint what it was. I figured that he was new and that is why he was so tentative about helping out when a firefighter or construction worker would come in with need of medical assistance. "Jane, Jared isn't pulling his weight," Jan whispered into my ear. "All he wants to do is sit around and either talk to us or chat with the workers that come in."

Jared had that way about him, he just eased himself into a situation and I just assumed he was working. "I guess I didn't realize that, Jan, he just seems to have placed himself as if he was always here! I'll chat with him about it and thanks for the heads up!"

Before I had a chance to say anything, Jared came up to me. "Sit down Jane, you seem so stressed. Let me give you a shoulder massage."

"Really Jared, that sounds good, but there is a lot of stuff that needs to be done," I mentioned.

"Five minutes, you can give me just five minutes, can't you? I have wanted to sit and chat with you for a while now. I have something I really want to tell you, and this will blow your mind!" he offered.

"Okay, five minutes, but then I have to get back. What do you want to tell me?"

"You know, it's as if I have known you all of my life! The minute I walked in the First Aid door I knew that I knew you!" he said.

"You knew me? I don't think so Jared. I have only known you a couple of days!"

"It's too bad you don't remember Jane, but I know that I have known you before. I'm pretty sure it was in a past life. What I do know is that you and I had a relationship at some point in history. Don't you feel that connection?" he asked.

"What? What are you saying?" I said searching his eyes.

"I just know it, I feel it. Can you get that? You know, past lives, like before you were born… previous lives," he insisted.

"Really? I find that very, very hard to believe Jared."

"You just don't believe enough. If you get to know me, you will eventually remember." He prodded. "I know that I loved you, in fact, the feeling is so strong that I know that I loved you more than your husband could ever love you!"

I stood up, and looked at him in disbelief. Who was this guy? This was just a bit too weird for me, I began to shake. "Listen Jared, it is an interesting story, but one that I truly do not believe in. I think it is time that we get back to work. Come on, there are a couple of new patients that need some medical assistance and we all need to get back to work."

"Don't worry, you will believe me eventually, I know you will, you have to, we have such a history together!" he said. "I'll help in a minute, I promise, but I have to go grab a bite to eat."

At that he walked out of the office. Wrapping my arms around me, I stood there with my mouth agape. *What had just happened*? I felt a shiver fill my body.

"Jane, what the heck is wrong? It looks like you saw a ghost!" Jan inquired.

"Well who knows, Jared thinks I did," I whispered.

"What are you talking about? What did he say to you?" she asked.

I sat there feeling numb and told her the bizarre story.

In the meantime, my lovely crew had surrounded me, supporting and worrying.

"I told you he was weird," Dan said. "Why don't we call headquarters and tell them he's a whack job?"

"He hasn't done a thing, just talked. I can handle that. If anything else happens, don't worry I will call HQ," I insisted.

"Promise?" Dan asked.

"I do and thanks for being there for me, I do appreciate it."

"Did you notice what he did?" Darlene asked. "He walked out of the room and didn't offer any medical help. Something is up with that guy, really Jane. This is odd."

"I'll keep my eyes open, I promise, now let's get back to work, okay?" I said. "I'm just fine, a bit shaken up but if I stay busy I'll be okay."

Little did I know, that was just the beginning. Each day he would come in and fabricate a story about the two of us. Some days I would find him sitting in the cafeteria, just staring at me. When I would catch his eye, he wouldn't look away, just continued to stare. Why I didn't report him sooner, I will never know.

"I will always know where you are Jane, I can just feel it," he said to me a few days later. "I can just visualize where you are and then I will be there, isn't that amazing? Can't you feel this bond between us?"

"Jared, please stop. This is really making me uncomfortable, do you get that? Why are you doing this to me," I pleaded.

"In time you will know," he said.

My group always walked me home as they were so concerned that he would appear out of nowhere. The final straw was when I was home that evening in my apartment, alone. My work cell phone rang. I just assumed that it was one of my medical staff that had a question.

"Jane, are you okay?" Jared asked.

"I'm fine, why? Is something wrong?"

"I just had this vision that something happened to you, something bad," he said.

"No Jared, everything is fine, I am just watching a movie. Please don't tie up this phone line as it is there so the staff can reach me if there is an issue at work!" I told him.

"Oh, good, as long as you are okay. I was just so worried!! Shall I come over to make sure everything is alright?" he asked.

"Please Jared, do not call, do not come over, okay? I'm doing fine. Please do not call again!" I pleaded.

I hung up the phone, checked the dead bolt on my door and made sure the curtains were pulled tight. I sobbed. *Why was this happening to me? Why couldn't he just leave me alone?*

I stopped outside the door of the main office at the Respite Center. Someone had said his name. Just his name and I had felt a cold wave rush over me. My heartbeat was in my throat. Did I want to go in? Did I want to know what they were talking about? Would it change anything, help the situation any?

I had been a volunteer now at Ground Zero for almost two months but the experience of meeting him had marred the many good things, incredible moments and people I'd gotten to know. It made me feel disheartened just to realize that. This had not been why I'd chosen to volunteer.

How could I help it that some man I'd never met before Ground Zero would choose to fixate on me! How could I have known that my talking to him would be misinterpreted to represent some divine intervention on his part?

I offered everyone the opportunity to talk. That was part

of my job, which was why I was there, to help people, to talk and to give first aid to the workers at the site.

But what had been a casual meeting by happenstance evolved into him showing up everyday, wherever I was. At first he even tried to pretend it was accidental, and for a while, I played along, hoping that by not making a big deal of it, perhaps he'd just move on. And now the calls. It was making me a nervous wreck. I never knew where he was going to show up or when.

Little did I realize, he just decided on his own to come to the First Aid center and he had no medical background (which I found out later).

I forced myself to turn the corner. Immediately, Phil and Darlene stopped talking. Both of them were staring at me. I could feel a flush of heat in my face. This was embarrassing and it wasn't my fault, I could feel myself getting angry.

"Hi Jane," they both said in unison, like stealthy co-conspirators.

"Phil, Darlene," I acknowledged.

"How's it going?"

"It's going fine, did I interrupt something?" I could hear it in my voice. It sounded curt. I was trying not to sound as agitated as I felt. Too late, I could see the look in Darlene's eyes. She looked as if I'd just slapped her.

"What do you mean?" she stuttered.

"Is something wrong?" Phil asked. Shoving his glasses farther on his nose, it gave him a very grandfatherly look.

"No, no," I brushed past them to get myself some coffee.

"Are you sure?" Darlene looked at me; there was fear in her eyes.

"What?" I asked. "Was Jared here again?"

"Yes," Phil answered. I rolled my eyes.

"Oh my God," I said setting my coffee mug down, Darlene squeezed my shoulder.

"I'm sorry Jane, we were just trying to figure out how to tell you when you came in," she said.

"Now what?" I asked. I could feel fear coursing through my veins like a slow poison.

"Jane I think you should sit down," Phil suggested.

"What's wrong Phil?" I asked knowing full well that by the look on his face, something was not okay. I'd known Phil long enough to know that he only got that look on his face when there was trouble or he was having difficulty in breaking some "hard" news to somebody. Since I knew I hadn't done anything wrong, it could only mean one thing: Hard news.

"Jared showed up again today for work, asking where you were. He says he has to talk to you," his eyes darted around the room, everywhere but focusing on me. A mix of emotions ran through me. A part of me was very angry, why should I be punished for what some unstable kook had done, while another part pumped pure fear through me. What did this mean? Would his little "gestures" escalate if I ignored him? Was I in danger???

"What did he say?" I found myself asking but not really wanting to know.

"Well, first of all, he wanted to know where you were," he cleared his throat. "Actually, he demanded to know where you were," Phil said, then he did look me in the eye. In his eyes, I saw worry and fear, two traits I had not seen coming from Phil before.

"We want you to know Jane, that we didn't tell him anything," Darlene chimed in.

I was speechless, numb. For a moment I didn't know how

to respond.

It made me feel guilty and in an odd way as if I should apologize, but for what? I hadn't done anything wrong. How could I possibly have known that my efforts to work with him to reach out to the survivors of Ground Zero could be so misconstrued by one man?

"Well, thank you for that," I said to them looking at Darlene. "I don't know what to say," I admitted. "Why is he doing this? This has got to stop!"

Phil touched my shoulder. It was as close to being comforting as he was capable of.

"It's not your fault Jane. We're just getting concerned for you. We don't want this to get out of hand," he said flatly. I was beside myself. What did that mean, "get out of hand"? Get out of hand for them or for me?

"Last night he called me at my apartment on the work cell phone. How did he get the number? He told me he just had a fear that something was wrong with me," I said. Reality began to settle over me, "Oh, now I really am concerned!" I exclaimed.

A wave of fear suddenly washed over me. Should I be scared? Was I in danger just because I was there trying to be supportive? I found myself shaking my head. Tears began to well up and I tilted my head back as to not have the tears fall down my face. I was trying to be so strong. I didn't want Phil or Darlene to see how emotional I really felt. I wanted to stay strong and in control, but Jared had just taken that away from me. Now I was getting scared.

"I've been thinking myself that maybe I need to not be so accessible, that if I wasn't here for awhile, maybe he'd lose interest," I said softly. Phil and Darlene both looked pathetic and forlorn.

"Exactly!" Phil said. "Jane you've done a wonderful job,

everyone loves you, we just don't want to see something happen to you. And with these kinda guys, it's better to just separate yourself," he said.

"I did ignore him, well, I mean I didn't encourage him," I told him.

"We know you didn't," Darlene said. "But he's just showing up over here all the time. It's making people nervous," she confessed.

"We have contacted headquarters about this and they are very worried for you, especially Jean. They want you to move out of the apartment. Darlene and Dan will help you and get you settled in the same hotel they are in, in midtown Manhattan," Phil said. "They are under strict orders from me not to leave your side!" He then said in a low voice, "you know we want you to stay here as you have been a huge asset, but everyone is concerned that this could escalate, you really should consider going home."

"I understand," I said, grabbing my coffee cup again. "I was thinking of going back home anyway, I miss my family, and it's been a long time since I've seen Gary. I am also tired of looking over my shoulders all the time, wondering when and where he will show up and what he will do," I said. They were both nodding their heads in unison.

"That's a great idea," Phil said.

"Thanks," I said. "So do you mind if I get to work then?"

"Of course not," Phil said looking a bit embarrassed. They both stepped back to allow me to walk past them. I shut the door feeling irritated and deflated that I had to leave.

But once in my office I was painfully aware of potential. Jared was not the kind of man who took no for an answer. It was time I went home. Mixed emotions were racing through my head. This was not the way I had intended to leave my assignment. I knew I had worked longer than the majority of the volunteers had, a total of six and a half weeks, but this way of leaving was leaving a bad taste in my mouth. It was unfair. Why did this man have to ruin it for me?

Darlene walked into the First Aid area after about ten minutes and said to me, "Jane, Phil wants you and I to go talk to Jean at Headquarters, he wants you to be able to tell your story to her. Is that okay, can we go now? Dan is still here and can hold down the fort and Donna and Sue are here this shift too, so there is plenty of coverage. You do know Phil is very worried, don't you?"

I nodded my head. I was feeling so defeated and had little energy to handle much of anything. I needed to rely on Darlene right now; she was my strength, my support.

We took the subway to the Red Cross Disaster Headquarters. "I'm not leaving your side, Jane. This has been traumatic and I don't want that guy sneaking up on you, so like it or not I'm your bodyguard right now," Darlene exclaimed. "For that I am grateful," I said giving Darlene's hand a squeeze.

We arrived at the Disaster Headquarters and immediately made our way to the medical area, which is where I always reported whenever I was in the building. Jean observed our walking in and stood up, walked over to me and much to my chagrin, gave me a very warm hug. She was not known for her calmer emotional side. "Phil phoned a while ago and filled me in. Jane, I want to hear from you exactly what is going on. From what Phil has told me, this is not a good situation at all. Let's go to a more private area so you can talk freely. Ben, would you mind taking over? I need to have some time with Jane. Darlene, please join us as I want your input too."

"First let me tell you that none of this is your fault," Jean said as we were taking our seats. "Tell me how ever on earth did this guy get into the Respite Center and how the heck did he end up in your First Aid Station? I did some checking and this guy has no medical experience."

"I can only try to piece this together, as it really makes no sense. I guess I am just too trusting of people. Jared just walked into my area saying he was reporting for duty. He told me he was a local volunteer and that First Aid was where he was to go. In hindsight, I should have checked his credentials. I didn't think I had to do that with the local volunteers as that had already been done at headquarters. I guess I learned my lesson! The hard way!"

"Did he offer first aid to anyone?" Jean inquired.

"Looking back on it, he didn't. He was awfully busy trying to impress all of us nurses with stories. I asked for him to help with things, but he really never did. He just would move to another side of the room and chit chat with the firemen or the nurses. After a while, I kind of forgot that he really wasn't doing any work. If I had, I would have talked to you sooner. I guess it is my fault, isn't it?"

"Oh, stop it Jane," Darlene stated with just a bit too much anger. "You couldn't control that guy, none of us could. Don't beat yourself up about it. You were the victim in this, he played you well. Tell Jean about his discussions with you, stating how he felt like he knew you in a past life."

"Okay, you're right Darlene. I just can't believe this is happening. This isn't how I want to leave New York, Jean!" I cried. "He spent way too much time talking to me whenever there was a lull in the First Aid station. I thought he was pretty out there when he told me how he believed in past lives and thought that we had known each other in another life. I laughed at him."

"Tell her about what he said about Gary," Darlene suggested, and then continued quickly. "Oh, I'll tell it. Do you know he told Jane that he just felt that he loved her in a past life, a kind of love that was much deeper than she had with Gary? He also said that he just seemed to know where Jane was all of the time and that even when they weren't together, he felt her presence and knew in his heart that he could find her anywhere she was."

I shuddered, remembering. My mind just wanted to shut down, I didn't want to think about this man, this man that had now given me such a sour taste in my mouth, making me uncomfortable to be anywhere alone. *Was he nearby hiding somewhere watching?*

"That's enough, as I know this is very painful for you. You too, Darlene. Don't worry, he won't be coming back to the Respite Center, we will make sure of that".

"I hope you won't tell him that he was reported by us!" I exclaimed.

"No, there is no worry there. We have decided on how to handle it, we will ask for his medical credentials, which we know he can't supply and then he will be banned from the Respite Center or from any work with Red Cross as he was not honest with us. He will never know that you have been worried about his interactions with you, I promise," Jean insisted.

"Here is what I want you to do, I want you to go to your apartment and gather your belongings. I plan to put you in the same hotel in Midtown where Darlene and Dan are both staying. Can you do that? We will make arrangements for you to get home to North Carolina tomorrow. How do you want to go, fly or take the train?"

"The thought of flying has no appeal to me, it freaks me out a bit, so I guess the train," I said despondently. "So now it's time to pack up and say goodbye I guess."

Darlene interrupted, "Jane, no worries, Dan and I aren't

leaving your side for a minute until we have you in your room at the hotel we are staying. You and I will take the subway back to the Respite Center, pick up Dan and then we will go over with you to your apartment and help you pack up all of your stuff. Sound good?"

"You did such a wonderful job at the Respite Center, Jane," Jean said. "You should be proud of yourself for all that you accomplished. Don't let this one person ruin it for you, understand? Also remember we are closing the Respite Center in two days, so really you were here basically the entire time the Respite Center was open."

"I do understand it's just hard, very hard," I said. Damn, I didn't want to cry but I couldn't help it. Darlene threw her arms around me and said, "Come on sister, let's get you packing!"

The goodbyes were difficult at the Respite Center. It especially was the staff at the First Aid Station that would pull at my heartstrings the most. I only had a few personal items in the room and was ready to head out the door, when the First Aid crew surrounded me. Darlene walked over and said, "We didn't have time to get you anything, Jane, but we all wanted to give you something that had meaning to you during your time here. We have the sign that was on the entrance door to the Fist Aid room to give you. You were the one here the longest and you are the one that deserves it." I watched a tear slowly trickle down her cheek as she handed me the laminated 8 x 11 sign. On it were the words *First Aid for Heroes*.

I took a deep breath and audibly swallowed hard. I looked around me, here were people I had known for such a short period of time, but they all had come to mean much more to me than just mere acquaintances. We had all experienced something larger than just a glancing friendship. These

160

individuals would remain close in my heart for years to come.

As I walked out the Respite Center doors, with Dan to my left and Darlene to my right I heard the big booming voice. "Hey little bit, thought you were going to leave without saying anything?" It was Phil. "I hate goodbyes, so I won't say it, but I just want to thank you. You helped me when you didn't need to, you know? You became my right hand person and were always there to help me with that darn computer that always gave me fits! What will I do?"

I laughed and reached out and said, "I know you don't like hugs, but darn it Phil, you are going to get one! I also don't want to say goodbye. I hope that someday down the road we can meet under much happier circumstances and have some well deserved laughs!" He held his arms out as if he didn't mind receiving that hug. I just held him, both of us filled with our own emotions.

"You are a class act my dear. Safe travels. Dan, Darlene take good care of this woman, she deserves a lot of TLC". He turned around and walked down the hall to his office and didn't look back.

CHAPTER 17

New Year's Resolution and Absolution

I returned from New York City two weeks after Thanksgiving, just in time to get ready for the many holiday celebrations. Life at Fort Bragg was always packed full of many social events to include many formal holiday balls, none that I was interested in attending. I forced myself to be part of it all as I knew I needed to get my mind off of Ground Zero. I felt as if I was just going through the military spouse motions. How does one pick up their life when everyone has moved on? The women were discussing which ball gown they would be wearing and I would be trying to stay in the present and not think about if another body was being pulled out of the pile.

I felt so alone, not part of the comings and goings of the military post. If only I could have stayed longer in New York. Why did Jared, my stalker, have to ruin everything for me? I was doing something so important and felt so insignificant returning to what people called 'the real world'. But everyone was enthralled with my story of being in New York at Ground Zero. I was frequently interviewed on television and on the radio and began giving speeches in the local area to local schools, community organizations and graduations. This would eventually grow overtime and within the next few months I would have many speaking engagements around the country. It helped talking about it; actually speaking became quite cathartic for me.

The major fact that I would be having Christmas with my grandson kept me going. JT was three years old and so full of excitement for the holiday. He was at the perfect age for believing and was full of wonderment.

My son Ian came home from NC State in Raleigh. It was delightful to celebrate the time with my family. Everyone was in the same state, my daughter Elizabeth and her husband James and of course JT. We were all going to be together. I needed them to be near, needed to feel something again. I made sure that we kept our many traditions our family has done over the years during holiday season and I was feeling pretty good about it. The Christmas Eve shrimp tree would be made and the Tomato Pudding would be served on Christmas day, as keeping with the traditions of many years past, my family's tradition. It was good to be around family, it was the rest of the world I wasn't so sure of!

Five days after Christmas the telephone rang, "Janie, its Melissa... Mom was admitted to the hospital today. I'm so worried. She seems so congested and is having a difficult time catching her breath. I guess the emphysema is getting the better of her. Can you come down?"

"Oh, no!" I said with anguish. As much as my mother challenged me, she was my mother and I loved her, through the good and the bad. "Let me throw a few things together and I will be there in about three hours, is that okay?"

"Hurry, it's not looking very good," she said.

I blindly went through the motions of throwing my clothes in a suitcase. I had no clue how long I would be there. Was it for a day, or for a week or what? Thankfully I was in still in the 'disaster' mode from Red Cross and kept my essentials packed and ready to go, as one never knows when you might be called. It came in handy. Gary stayed home and told me to call him immediately when I arrived. He said that he would be on his way as soon as he could make arrangements at work.

Less than an hour later I was throwing my suitcase in the car. Thank goodness my sister was only a short two hours from where we lived and the hospital, a local community hospital, was very close to her home. I don't remember the drive much, I just kept thinking *hang on Mom, I will be there soon. I need to see you! We need to patch up things, I don't want to leave things the way that they are!*

The next few days were a monumental blur. New Years went by with hardly a thought that 2002 was upon us. They suggested that Mom should be intubated which meant putting her on a respirator and giving her lungs a chance to heal as much as possible, to put her in a drug induced coma. This was incredibly serious and our concerns were whether the small community hospital would be the best option for her. Though her care was excellent, we felt that she needed the expertise of the larger teaching hospital on the other side of Richmond, about twenty-five miles away. We decided a transfer needed to be done.

The ambulance arrived to take Mom during the middle of a major winter snow storm. Time was of the essence and we knew we had to get her transported no matter what Mother Nature had in store for us. The twenty-five miles seemed as if it were 250 miles as it snowed heavily the entire way with accumulations of over eight inches. We crept along just behind the ambulance in our vehicles hoping that the weather didn't have any other plans for us.

"Only time will tell," the pulmonologist, Dr. Ortiz, informed us. "We need to give those lungs of hers a rest. Is she still a smoker?"

"No, she stopped right after our Dad passed away, about twelve years ago," I said wincing, remembering how angry I was that she wouldn't give it up until then. Did my Dad's passing have anything to do with her constant smoking? Now look what it had done to her!

"How many years did she smoke?" he asked.

Melissa piped in, "at least fifty years I think."

"Unfortunately the damage is done; she will most likely be

on some form of oxygen the rest of her life, even *if* we can get her through this event," he shrugged, "and that is a big *if*."

My brother, Martin asked, "How long, Doctor, will she be in this coma? Are we talking days or weeks? I know that Mom has a 'no heroics' listed in her medical directive."

"At this point it is not heroics, as she consented to have this done. Again, time will tell, but my guess is that in two or three days we will try to wean her from the machine to see how she does. I'm hoping the lungs will recover enough," the doctor said. "But just to be clear, if we do get her through this, and she goes into a rehabilitation facility to get her strength back, we are not talking a huge amount of time that your mother has left. My guess, if we can get her through this, we are talking less than two years."

"We will take what we can get," we all said in unison.

I barely left her side, only to go to my sister's house to sleep. I had some time with her, maybe… and I knew that it was a BIG maybe. Our relationship over the years had always been challenging. I needed to get to the bottom of it and understand why it was that way. Why did she always criticize, why did she always put me behind my sister as an after-thought? Was this all my imagination?

I reached for her hand, so limp, so unresponsive and said, "Oh Mom, my New Year's resolution is to figure us out, make us love each other, make you proud of me. Please, please give me that. I want this so badly." Tears began to flow, tears of sadness seeing my mother in such a vulnerable way and sadness over our 'not so close' relationship we had held for so very many years.

I realized that in the last several days I had barely thought about Ground Zero. That thought hit me like a ton of bricks. I felt guilty, shouldn't I be thinking about everyone in New York, thinking about what must be going on? But then I realized that this time with my mother trumped over everything else I had been experiencing since 9/11, this time was ever so precious and fragile.

As the saying goes, "Time heals" and it did in more ways than one. I will forever be grateful that I was given the gift of having my mother back in my life.

The ventilator was removed gradually and Mom's lungs slowly rebounded. A huge sigh and then a big chuckle went around the room when she opened her eyes and asked for a coke! With a comment like that, we knew that she was on the mend. Three days on a respirator left our mother extremely weak. We knew that she could not return to her own home, but just as Dr. Ortiz said, a rehab facility would help get her strength back.

Her feistiness came back with a vengeance when she heard she had to go to rehab. "You are just trying to put me away, get rid of me, aren't you?"

"Mom, you know that isn't true, you heard Dr. Ortiz, you are weak and need to regain your strength!" Melissa pleaded.

"Oh it's just a nursing home and I'm sure you want to take me there to rot!" she insisted.

"Come on Mom. I'm going to be visiting you all the time, we all are. The doctor said that this nursing home has a stellar physical therapy department. I think you are going to like it," I suggested.

"Well, I know I am very weak, but I am NOT staying there forever. You have to promise me that. I have to get home!"

"We've been talking about that Mom and Janie and Gary have offered to have you come to their house at Fort Bragg once you get your strength back," said Melissa.

"So I'm not ever going back to my house?" she

whimpered.

"Of course you are, we know it is going to take a while to regain your strength to where you were before you went into the hospital. With Melissa teaching, no one would be there for you during the day if you went back to your house. But I am not working now and I am not going back to New York so I have time to be there for you. Let me do that for you, okay? We have the perfect room for you at our house that's on the main floor so you won't have to go up any of the stairs. It even has its own bathroom too!" I said searching her eyes, hoping to see some positive affirmation.

"But you and Gary need your own life, you don't need an invalid."

"We need you, okay? We are going to make this work, but right now, let's deal with the task at hand and get you settled into the rehab center," I said smiling, knowing that I had won this mini battle.

Everything went according to plan and as we expected, she hated the rehab facility and hated her roommate. She refused to have her dinner in the dining hall because as she informed us, there were *old* people in there. What she loved was going to physical therapy as she became their prized pupil. She loved each of them as much as they loved her and pretty soon all of them were on a first name basis. Her only sadness leaving the rehab facility six weeks later, was saying goodbye to the wonderful Physical Therapy department.

I got my wish; she rallied, made it through a terrible ordeal in the hospital, weaned herself off of the ventilator and thrived with physical therapy and love from her family. Now it was my turn, my turn to make things right between us. How much time did I have?

CHAPTER 18

Picking up the Pieces

So much had happened in the last month that I found myself feeling jet lagged between two states and three separate ways of life; the life on the Army base, my life after 9/11, and then the return home with my mother in tow, making it now impossible for me to return to Ground Zero.

Physically I had returned to Gary, to some sense of normalcy that I had known before the event. But in my heart, my emotions, and my mind, I was still held captive by the experiences of the past few months.

The images on the Teddy Bear Wall, the ruin and debris and recovery of all those lost on that fateful day were an intrinsic slideshow that would never be erased. It had been permanently etched in my brain just as the reality of that day would remain a stain on America's history throughout all time.

As a result of my vigilance, my mother, who was now rather fragile after her hospital and rehab ordeal had come to stay with us during her recovery period. I looked at my mother sitting in the recliner in the living room by the fireplace, next to a collection of family photos.

I focused on her face, pale and sleeping. I stared at the photographs showing me smiling with my sister and brother and one picture of my mother, reflecting a happiness that did not belong to my memories of youth. Where was *that* woman? Where had she been when I desperately needed her all those years growing up hearing over and over again how I wasn't successful enough, pretty enough. Why was she ill? Why now?

A wave of anger and resentment washed over me. My mother had never been an easy woman to please. But the woman I remembered being so critical of me seemed subdued now. And yet, on some level, she was still in my life, just as I had always been in hers.

It was years ago but yet it felt fresh, the sting of lost years, wasted opportunities. The many, many times I had watched my mother dote on my sister and living vicariously through her. What was wrong with me? Why didn't she ever care about my accomplishments? When I thought about all the times that I had pushed myself to be the best in my class, to keep my grades up all to no avail, she could easily let it all make me bitter. I got tired of living life through my sister's shadow. How many times had I watched my mom bake and bake only to suddenly proclaim she had a headache, and then retire to her bedroom? Mom always had headaches.

I grew up in a small town in Ohio, Cuyahoga Falls, located about 30 miles south of Cleveland. It was a wonderful area to raise a family. If only Mom would have been happier while we were there. Raising four children pretty much by herself had to be a challenge, as my father worked long hours in his job. We all lived for the weekends when Dad could play with us and take us to the Gorge and Virginia Kendall Park for long hikes. Mom would usually come along and prepare a big breakfast prior to our hikes. Then she would sit at the picnic table and smoke cigarettes while we were off hiking. Looking back on it, she must have been lonely, very lonely. As a child I was oblivious to that concept. I wish I could go back in time and have a re-do.

"Finally, you're proud of me," I muttered, unaware that my mother was awake.

Unexpectedly she lifted her head, opened her eyes and peered at me. Even with the tuffs of white hair and her newly acquired diminutive appearance, I could feel the weight of those eyes.

"Did you say something?" she asked.

"No," I said too quickly. Our eyes met.

"Don't mutter Jane, it's so unbecoming," my mother said.

"Right." I said to myself. "No, I was just checking in on you. Do you need anything?" I asked.

She looked up. It was clear from the look on my face that she didn't believe me but for reasons only she knew, she didn't say anymore. Instead she closed her eyes and within a few minutes was once again softly snoring.

I felt like I'd just dodged a huge bullet. As I busied myself cleaning up the kitchen and straightening up around the living room and dining room, my thoughts returned to more unpleasant moments. I chastised myself for dwelling on the negative but couldn't quite get myself to let go.

A poem I had written long, long ago came to mind. I thought about the words, so profound to be written by a child. It made me aware how long this barrier between us had existed.

A garden of flowers
All in a long row
At the end is one flower
No different than the rest
Just left out
While the others bloom
It fades

I set down the duster on the end table by the recliner. I watched my mother, seemingly so peaceful, now. But the heavy memories stayed with me, hung in the air like a wisp of smoke.

"Can we finally have a truce mom?" I said softly, and then looked up to see if her eyes were open again, but they weren't. Only her soft, steady snoring answered me.

I know she slept through my plea, but somehow I felt that she must have heard me. Our relationship from that point on began to change, change for the better. There was no aha moment that came, it wasn't an instant change by any means. It happened though but it was gradual, ever so gradual, almost impossible to detect. I cannot pinpoint the exact day or the week that I saw the change in her, but it happened. Was it my Mom that changed? Maybe it was me? Or was it both of us that finally called the truce? I will never know, but somehow the bitterness slowly faded and was replaced by more acceptance, caring and love, on both of our parts. For me the pain and anger have diminished over time leaving behind a memory. We smiled more, respected each other more and enjoyed being with each other those last eighteen months of her life.

I got my wish.

CHAPTER 19

Hometown Hero and the POTUS
March 2002

I was up early that morning, for some reason, I just felt restless. So after doing the dishes and putting in a load of laundry, I let myself have a cup of coffee.

No sooner had I sat down when the phone rang. I made a mad dash to answer it before it would wake up my Mom. She had been staying with us for a while now, but her health was still fragile so she was still recuperating at our home. By now it was nearing the middle of the day, but with my mother's health being so weak, she was still resting. It was not unusual for her to take several naps during the course of a day.

"Hello?" I whispered.

"Jane?" A woman's voice asked.

"Yes, this is Jane," I answered, wondering who was calling.

"Hi, this is Jackie Jones and I am on staff at the White House. Cathy from volunteer services at Fort Bragg gave me your name. You are one of our candidates for meeting with the POTUS when he comes into town in a couple of weeks. The other two volunteers are from the Fayetteville community."

My mind drew a blank. *Okay now I felt really stupid, I had never heard the term POTUS, but learned pretty quickly that it stood for President of the United States.*

"Excuse me, did you say, the White House?" I stammered trying to grasp why they'd be calling *me*. She tried to suppress a giggle and lightheartedly informed me that yes it was true, she did work at the White House.

"Yes, Jane, I work in Washington, DC at the White House.

There are two other candidates that we are interested in and will interview, but to tell you the truth, you have the most amazing volunteer experience and I think this is exactly what President Bush would like."

President Bush would like? The words buzzed through my brain. I was awestruck. Was I really hearing her correctly, was this some sort of dream I was having? This kind of stuff just didn't happen, at least not to me. Before I could pinch myself to get over the shock Jackie began firing questions at me.

"I would like you to give me an overview of your time working in New York City after 9/11," she said. "What made you decide to go? Were you asked to go, did you decide on your own and why would you want to do that?"

"No one asked me to go," I said. "It was just something that I felt very compelled to do. I was volunteering at the American Red Cross at Fort Bragg and was busy answering the phone."

She interrupted, "Answering the phone? Who was calling?"

"Americans that just wanted to help in any way that they could, mostly they wanted to donate money," I said. "I just knew that even though that was an important thing, it wasn't enough for me, I wanted to give more somehow, and I needed to go to help. It didn't matter where it was, Washington, DC, Pennsylvania or New York City. I knew that being a registered nurse I could offer more." For a moment there was silence, as if she were thinking about what I'd just said.

"Well how long did it take before they sent you? Was it immediately?" she prodded.

"Oh no, I had to go through classes in Disaster training," I informed her.

"How long were you in New York?" she asked.

"A total of almost seven weeks and I was right at Ground Zero working in one of the Respite Centers," I said.

"Well this is very interesting and I am sure we will be talking a lot more in the near future. I just needed a basic background on why the Fort Bragg volunteer office recommended you so highly. Now I know!" she exclaimed. "Within the next couple of days you will be hearing from us, if you are selected. Really though, this is just a formality, I believe I found our volunteer!"

I put the receiver down and just stood there, numb. *What the heck? Could this all really be true or was this someone's idea of a joke?* I had to know so I decided to immediately call the volunteer office and talk to Cathy, but the phone rang again. This time it was Cathy, her voice bubbling over with emotion.

"Jane, the White House just called me!" she gushed, "Can you believe it?"

I chuckled then told her that I absolutely did believe it as I had just gotten off the phone with them too. Now I knew that it wasn't a joke, this *was real*!

"I think your chances are good Jane!" she chattered on excitedly. "I surely said some great things about you and I'm pretty sure you are going to be the one. I guess our President is coming to town to talk to the soldiers and he has started some new program and he is meeting with volunteers around the county. This is just amazing!!" Cathy exclaimed.

It was amazing. And so surreal to me, all the things I'd done, I'd done out of a need to do my utmost. It had never occurred to me that my own sense of duty would warrant gratitude or be acknowledged beyond a simple 'thank you'.

In the midst of all my own zeal over the news I hadn't noticed that my mother had wandered out from her room. She looked diminutive and confused.

"Janie, what is going on? You sound so excited, what has happened? Is it Gary?" she asked concerned.

"No Mom, it's not Gary this time," I assured. "It's about me and I have a feeling the next few days you are going to be a busy lady answering the phone when I am not here!" I said smiling.

"What? How come? Well tell me what it is please!" she said, starting to smile too.

"Mom that was the White House on the phone, the President of the United States wants to meet me!" I couldn't believe I was saying those words, it was unbelievable.

"He wants to meet *you*? Why?" she asked.

"Well it is a shock to me too, but I guess he and his staff are interested in the work that I did while I was in New York City at Ground Zero".

It was if a light went on in my mother's brain that showed in her expression. Suddenly she did an about face.

"Well Janie, you really do deserve that recognition! I am so pleased for you and so proud of you!" She declared.

Had I really heard the words I had been wanting for so many years to hear? Did she really just say them or did I imagine it? Had she really said she was proud of me, her black sheep daughter?

It had only taken fifty years and a call from the White House to make it happen, but alas, it had happened. My mother had finally seen me as one of her daughters, recognized me, for my own merit.

Hey, I didn't care how, I'd gotten here I was just overjoyed that I'd finally heard the words! Without giving it a second thought, I threw my arms around her and gave her a big hug and a kiss on the cheek. That did it. She grinned from ear to ear!

In that moment something had been forever changed between the two of us. I would never be like my sister, but for once, at last, I was okay just being me.

Indeed things did start to pop. Within twenty four hours I received the phone call stating that I was the one they'd picked to meet President Bush. Then they informed me that the President would be arriving at the Fayetteville Airport on March 15. I was to be there early in the morning prior to his arrival for my briefing.

I was further instructed that after the meet and greet at the airport I would be part of the motorcade going to the Cumberland County Arena. It would be there that the President would give his speech.

It didn't take long for the word to get out that I was selected by the White House. As I had predicted Mom's job suddenly got very busy. In fact things got so chaotic that she had to keep a clip board, paper, pen and the phone with her all the time.

On it went each day that by the time I would get home from my volunteer meetings, Mom had a list of people I was to call back to set up interviews.

"Janie, ABC in Raleigh called and you *need* to call them right back, they have called five times!" I chuckled to myself; this was so good for her, as it really gave her a purpose. She was just glowing with excitement.

Finally the infamous day of March 15th 2002 arrived and as directed, I made my way to the airport in Fayetteville to the waiting area and paced nervously in a small sectioned off area as I waited to be briefed by the President's staff. I was not alone. There were many dignitaries there: Mayors, military generals and Elizabeth Dole.

I especially wanted to talk to her since she had been a past President of the Red Cross. Since I was there because of the

Red Cross, it seemed important to me. Unfortunately, she was too busy meeting with everyone else so I never got the opportunity to talk to her. I was, however, able to get my picture taken with her and it was supposed to be sent to me, but unfortunately it never was.

I was told that we were to wait on the tarmac when Air Force One landed and then we were instructed to stand in a single line so that when he got off the plane, he could talk to each individual person. I was told to stand in the very back, the last person in a long line.

I could feel my heart pounding. Oh it was very exciting! I was going to meet the President of the United States! What an auspicious day! The sky was clear and the day was sunny and warm as we all watched the plane come in.

I could feel my heartbeat in my ears and it felt like my stomach had done a complete flip flop! Once the plane taxied into place we were all ushered out to the tarmac. There were a lot of important people there which translated to include a massive amount of press.

President Bush got off the plane and began shaking hands with each person. Because there were so many people, I was sure he wouldn't have time to come and talk to me.

Suddenly one of his aids came up to me and asked that I to move under the wing of the plane. She said that "when the POTUS finished shaking hands he would come over" to meet me.

I moved over by the plane, feeling very odd to be there all by myself. It made me feel as though I was sticking out like a sore thumb. I watched as the President shook hands with the last person. His car was right there waiting for him. My heart sank, I thought *NO, please don't go to the car, you are supposed to come and talk to me!* Almost as if on cue, he immediately turned and began walking towards me smiling and extending his hand.

"Jane, I want to thank you for all of your volunteer work that you did at Ground Zero!" he said.

"Thank you," I think I managed to say, but I honestly can't remember.

"It was a very difficult time for everyone and you came to help, that is amazing," he said. He handed me a baseball cap that had *USA Freedom Corps* on its brim and I gave him a t-shirt from Fort Bragg volunteers. (USA Freedom Corps was officially established on January 30, 2002, by President Bush to help find opportunities for every American to start volunteering both within the United States and abroad.)

As I got my thoughts back I said, "It was just something I felt that I really needed to do!"

He said, "The media is going nuts here, I guess that they want a picture of us. Are you ready to smile?" He put his arm around my back and turned me in the direction of the media. I thought, *hmmm he put his arm around me, can't I do the same?* So I did!

In a second it was over and he was escorted to his car while I was escorted into one of the other cars behind him and we all went in the motorcade to the arena. It was a fairly short drive, though I don't remember much of it. Pinch me, was all I kept thinking.

As we were walking into the Arena a woman came up to me smiling warmly and said, "Thank you, Jane, for all of your work in New York City." I did a double take; I had seen that face all over the news! It was the Secretary of State, Condoleezza Rice! This day was turning out to be so incredible. From there we were all escorted into the arena and given special seats to sit in.

I had thought I was there just to hear the President speak, which would have been quite a thrill on its own. I truly had no idea what was coming.

The President's speech began; he talked to the soldiers of Fort Bragg and told them, "We're in for a long struggle. Thousands of terrorists have been brought to justice. But I want you to know, my fellow citizens, we will not relent. We will not slow down until the threat of global terrorism has been destroyed. We're working hard to make sure the homeland is secure."

He continued with, "You know, the true strength of our country is much greater than our military. The true strength of America are the hearts and souls of loving American citizens. And we have an obligation in our free society to work to make our society as compassionate and as kind as it can possibly be."

"Today, I had the honor when I landed here to meet Jane Davis. Where are you, Jane? There she is." *I stood up,* surprised they were singling me out. "Jane, thank you. (Then there was applause.) Don't clap yet until you hear about her. She's the wife of Col. Gary Matteson of Fort Bragg.

The reason I mention Jane is because she is an example of what I'm talking about, about the strength of the country. Right after September the 11th, she left North Carolina to volunteer at Ground Zero in New York City. (There was more applause.) Nobody had to tell Jane. There wasn't a government edict, there wasn't a telegram from Washington, D.C., directing her to go to Ground Zero; she followed her heart. She knew it was the right thing to do."

"It's the Jane Davis's that really defined America for the world to see."

The point of this part of his speech was to discuss his new volunteer program USA Freedom Corps. "If you want to help," he said, "you can get on the Internet and dial up usafreedomcorps.gov and see. If you want to be involved there are all kinds of ways."

The speech was just about over, but the people around me were all complimenting me and patting me on the back. I was just shaking. I truly couldn't believe this was happening.

It seemed that as soon as it had begun, it was over and I was heading home in my car. Unbeknownst to me, my mother had heard the speech on TV and was full of jubilation when I got home.

After the broadcast the phone began ringing all day long. I even got a call from my dear friend Joan, in Washington State.

"Jane, I was watching the news and heard the President's speech and pretty soon I heard him mention you! It is so well deserved, congratulations!" I was speechless.

Apparently his speech was broadcast nationwide! I had no idea.

Life eventually began to settle down and return to normal for me. My five minutes of fame was over. But I will never forget that special day in March of 2001. It was an honor and a privilege to meet the President of the United States. An honor few will ever know. But an honor that greatly impacted me and forever changed my life.

To me it was like a giant affirmation that the choice I'd made all those months before had been right. My intention had been to help those in need, but if my helping helped to serve a greater cause in this nation, then I was more than happy to be there. It was my *duty*.

CHAPTER 20

Out of the Fire-Moving on

Caring for my mother was my way to hide from the world, keep me in my protective shell. I could be with her and forget about almost everything else. Watching her progress warmed my heart, but also saddened me as I knew it was only a matter of time that she would be returning to her home. We would both get our independence back. I didn't know if I was ready for that. Her health did rapidly improve and the day finally came that she was strong enough to return home. Such mixed emotions went through me that day driving her back. It was an emotional struggle to have her leave and a worry whether she would be okay. I knew that she would be okay as my sister Melissa only lived a mere seven houses away from her. She would be able to arrive at Mom's house at a moment's notice. Melissa would shop for her, cook if needed and be there to take her to her doctor's appointment and do all of the things that she did so well. Melissa worried so much about our Mom and would do anything she could to make Mom as comfortable as possible. Mom was in very good hands. Her last words to me were, "I love you, Janie." Ah, this was music to my ears.

I was thankful that we were going to be moving to Washington D.C. It was a good decision and where my heart was tugging at me to go. I had a burning need to be closer to the hub of what was going on in our nation's capital.

I stood in front of my dresser and the larger wall mirror, looking at myself. The face was the same, but inside I knew I was different.

Gary came in and slipped his arms around me. I smiled.
"Hey," I said.
"Hi beautiful. What are you doing?"
"Just thinking," I answered as I turned into him.

"Uh oh," he teased. I chuckled.

"Hey!"

"What about?" Gary prodded.

For a minute I was silent. I needed to choose my words carefully. I did not want Gary thinking that *my* restlessness was a reflection on him.

He noticed my quiescence and tilted my chin upward. Our eyes met. I knew this gesture well. It was Gary's way of trying to be understanding.

"What's wrong?" he said softly.

"I think I'm just pensive about moving – again," I said barely looking at his eyes.

"Jane?"

I moved back. Under the weight of Gary's gaze it was hard not to surrender the truth. And yet my own reticence made me continue.

"I haven't even packed any of "my" things yet!" I confessed with a hint of anger in my voice. Hearing the inflection startled us both. Gary stepped back to look at his me. I started shaking my head and waving my hand dismissively. "No, no, no. I'm okay," I assured.

"Are you?"

"Yes, I am," I said again. "It's just that when I was volunteering at Ground Zero I felt so alive. I was needed. I knew my work was important. You know? And then these months of taking care of my Mom too has given me a purpose. The speaking engagements make me realize that this could be a new avenue for me, but with moving, no one will know me!

You know what is going to be the most difficult? I have to say goodbye to JT! How can I look that little guy in the eye and say goodbye? Then there are our kids! Oh, I just can't leave everyone; things are changing awfully fast right now."

I looked at him.

Gary had always been a supportive spouse but this was a side of me he wasn't accustomed to seeing. I could see from the look on his face that he was a bit confused about what kind of a response I wanted from him.

I wanted to say *just be yourself* but I didn't. Something within me, perhaps in that single moment of uncertainty made it impossible for me to do.

"Everything you do is important. And all of the Fort Bragg organizations need you. JT will still have you Jane, as will the kids, we are not going to be that far away and by the way I need you!" he told me.

I raised a hand to his cheek and held it there for a few seconds while I looked at him. Then I gave him a small smile.

"That's not what I meant. But thank you," I said opening one of the dresser drawers and extracting some of my clothes. Gary watched me take stack after stack as I formed a pile of the bed.

"Don't you know how important you are?" he asked looking a tad uncomfortable.

"It's not the same Gary. Your work at the hospital is where you thrive. This is where I thrive. You know?" I paused. For a few moments we remained, looking at each other.

"Honey if you want to do work like that I won't get in your way," he said.

My eyes welled up. I loved this man. And his words were just an affirmation of why I married him. He understood me in ways that others did not, certainly beyond the comprehensions of my own mother. That knowledge saddened me.

"I know," I gave him a hug.

"Hope you do know," he pressed.

"Yes," I repeated.

"D.C. is going to be a new start for us. I'll have my work but you can do whatever you want. You don't have to run a bunch of meetings and groups if your heart's not in it. I'm just so proud of you and everything you do," he told me.

"I know," I said almost in a whisper before the tears fell. How could I explain to him what this meant to me, this nebulous quest that even I had not defined? Only that when I had been in the arms of the work, I had felt a vigilance and excitement that made my blood course through my body with a different intensity that I had not known before?

"Honey," Gary wiped away my tears. I felt my face sink into the curve of Gary's shoulder, tears flowed freely. Where was all this emotion coming from?

"I'm alright," I choked a little raspy and short of breath. "You're right, it'll be a new beginning, just what we need," I told him.

"You do know that, the packers will do all of that don't you?" he joked.

"I know, and you tell me that every single time we move, but I just need to have some control of this situation," I laughed.

"Okay. Then we'll go to dinner?" he continued.

"Of course," I said a little too quickly. We looked at each other. As if Gary could sense my fear, he gave me a quick peck and left the bedroom.

"Thank you," I said with a whisper.

CHAPTER 21

Somebody to the Unknown

We knew that Gary's command of the hospital at Fort
Bragg was only for two years and we would be moving
sometime in the summer of 2002. It was a feeling of mixed
emotions, as it always was when we knew we were off to
a new assignment. This would be 18th move for us since
meeting Gary in 1976. It was always a feeling of excitement
and fear heading out again, fear of the unknown. The great
thing about military life and moving is that we always
seemed to know someone at the new assignment. Being
associated with the military made everyone say, "It's a small
world."

Gary's next assignment was going to be Army Materiel
Command in Northern Virginia. We took a long weekend
up to Northern Virginia to begin looking for our next home.
Our Fort Bragg home had so much character and history
and I knew that I probably would never again move into a
home like that. But alas, it was time to move on and put
those memories on hold. With only a few days to search, we
knew that we were in store for a busy weekend. It seemed as
if we looked at thousands of homes, but it was probably no
more than twenty. We finally found just what we had been
searching for in Springfield, Virginia. It was a white two
story colonial with 4 bedrooms and 3½ baths with a beautiful
piece of property.

The last months at Fort Bragg were a very busy time with
farewell parties for those of us that were moving and Change
of Command ceremonies, to include Gary's. Gary's change
of command was a big event, for the hospital, the military
community and especially for Gary. This was the end of
his largest command and was for him, a culmination of his
military life. After attending many of these over the years,

hundreds I would imagine, I will tell you it is different when it is your loved one that is the one leaving and moving on with his career. There is such an emotional charge in the air.

Most of these COC's, as they are called, are held on the parade field. Our two children, Elizabeth and Ian were there along with James, our son-in-law, and JT. We were all seated at the dais; I was sitting next to the Commanding General's spouse.

The change of command ceremony is steeped in a rich history and tradition. One of the first things that happens is the outgoing commander's spouse (that would be me) is given a bouquet of red roses. The roses symbolize my *'devotion, dedication and tireless efforts to the soldiers and families of the hospital'*, and the incoming commander's spouse is given a bouquet of yellow roses which is from the soldiers of the hospital to welcome her.

The tradition of the change of command dates back to the reign of Frederick the Great of Prussia, during the 18th century. Each unit had and still has their individual organizational flag, with specific color arrangements and symbols specific to the unit. The flag represents loyalty and trust.

The flag was passed from Gary, the outgoing commander, to the incoming commander. The tradition is that with the passing of the flag, the soldiers will witness their new commander assuming his/her position and therefore will hold the soldiers' allegiance.

Watching the soldiers standing at attention, to include Gary, on the field and hearing the Fort Bragg Army Band play, gave me such a sense of pride. Tears were hard to hold back at that point, I was proud of my husband, but sad that the two years had flown by so fast. Yes, I was eager to move on, but this was an emotional event and millions of thoughts

197

kept popping into my brain as the ceremony continued. *Am I ready to leave? How do I say goodbye to my friends and especially my family. Will I make new friends? What was out there for me in Washington, DC? Would I be able to make a success of myself there? Can I continue to speak and will anyone listen up there? I want to continue to be a somebody; it's my turn to shine. Gary has had his career and I wanted something for me.* I felt like I was in a fog but then realized that Gary was speaking to everyone saying wonderful words, sharing his experience to everyone about his command of the hospital and thanking individual people, to include me and his family. I felt guilty, as I was thinking about me and not about the affect this was having on him. My heart went out to him.

It seemed as if the ceremony flew by and the Army Band was playing the Army song signifying the end of the ceremony. It was over and Gary was no longer in command. That had to be an odd feeling for him, as we were still living on the military post. We were pretty sure that the hospital would be his last command, but he felt strongly that he was not yet ready to end his military career. The military had been so good to Gary, given him so many wonderful opportunities. It just wasn't time to say goodbye to the Army. It was the same for me as all of the committees had ended for the summer and all I had to do now was get our quarters ready for the move and wait for the many farewell dinners to attend, including our own.

Saying Goodbye

How does one say goodbye to an assignment that was so inspiring? The friends we made, the connections, the activities, the family events and even the experiences we all shared during 9/11 made those two years unforgettable. Now it was time for all of the parties and saying goodbye to so many people that were also moving away to their next assignments. Our calendars were full those last few weeks. There were coffees, luncheons, dinners, award ceremonies. The list kept going. The highlight of the farewells, for us, was Gary's farewell dinner from the hospital held at the Officer's Club at Fort Bragg. Many people that didn't work at the hospital were also included, especially our closest friends and our family. Elizabeth, James and Ian were able to come as were my sister, Melissa and her husband Mark.

There were many gifts and farewell speeches given that night. It was an evening of such mixed emotions for both Gary and me. The kind words that were shared gave me such a sense of pride, for being part of such a great community of Fort Bragg. For having wonderful friends and co-volunteers, for the hospital that supported both Gary and me beyond words and of course the pride in my husband for making such a great contribution to the Fort Bragg community just filled my heart.

The evening was winding down and I was feeling quite emotional, on the verge of tears, tears of happiness and sadness of saying goodbye. "Jane, can you please come up front, I have something to give you," Brigadier General William Fox said. I know that happens a lot during these events that the wife gets called up to the front to be thanked for her contributions so I wasn't too surprised, but I had no idea that the words that were to be spoken next would be so heartfelt. I tried to regain my emotional composure before going up front and standing next to BG Fox.

"Jane, you have gone above and beyond in your contributions to this community. Not only have you been an outstanding volunteer in our Fort Bragg community, holding leadership roles in the many programs on our post, but you also selflessly gave of yourself to volunteer in New York City during such a terrible time in our history. It is my/our honor to present to you the Dr. Mary E. Walker award," he said.

Dr. Mary E. Walker Award Citation

UNITED STATES ARMY
MILITARY DISTRICT OF WASHINGTON
Dr. Mary E. Walker Award

Is Presented To

Jane Davis

as an outstanding military spouse for demonstrating dedicated and exemplary volunteerism, that improved the quality of life for soldiers and their families.

Dr. Mary E. Walker

Dr. Mary E. Walker is the only woman in the United States history to receive the Medal of Honor. She became one of the first women physicians in the country in 1855. At the outbreak of war in 1861, Dr. Walker was denied a commission as an Army surgeon because of her gender. She served as an unpaid volunteer in Washington, in various military camps, and in a hospital for Indiana troops. She was instrumental in establishing an organization which aided needy women who came to Washington to visit wounded relatives. She served as a field surgeon on a volunteer basis, rendering assistance at tent hospitals in Virginia. She was eventually appointed as an assistant surgeon and assigned to the 52d Ohio Regiment. With immense courage and bravery rarely matched, Dr. Walker demonstrated her dedication to the American cause at great personal risk. She consistently discounted personal injuries and great hardships to care for others. She was captured and held a prisoner of war for four months before being freed in a prisoner exchange. Through her actions, Dr. Mary E. Walker set the standards for helping to improve soldiers' quality of life for generations.

I went up front to receive my award. I was so honored to be receiving it that I couldn't stop smiling. This was a great award, but meant so much more to me (though the award was great) knowing that people took their time to make this happen, that they thought enough of me to give me that award, that part was priceless. I had received many volunteer awards and recognition over the years while Gary was in the military. The Heidelberg Star, The FORSCOM Commander's Award, Volunteer of the Year Award, plus many Red Cross Awards, Unit awards and the Iron Mike Award, all topped off by meeting and getting acknowledged by President Bush.

Every one of these awards and recognitions have meant so much to me and earned a special place in my heart. But I knew these days were ending, and with it, that this would be my last award with the military as we were moving on and Gary's military career was coming to a close. I graciously thanked everyone including BG Fox and just let the tears fall. Gary came over and gave me a kiss and said, "Jane you deserve this, I am so proud of you".

The evening was winding down and people were beginning to leave. I knew deep in my heart that many of these people that were there that night, I would never see again. As the saying goes, People come in and out of your life for a reason. It made me think of the poem that was read at my baby brother, Scott's funeral, which follows:

It seems where ever I go,
People come into my life
Or go out of it...leaving me
Only a memory, touching me
Where I can feel it and
I wasn't through knowing them

How do I halt my life to gather
And keep those around me that
I've known and loved?
How do I know I am seeing you
For the last time?
And how do you keep fairy tales
From losing their magic?

And so ends an exciting chapter
Of our lives, but also begins another chapter.
And though we must part,
We know we can always return to keep
Fondly through the gold bound leaves
Of our memory.

For fairy tales are the happiest
Stories we read,
And good books are made of little chapters.
There remains so much to say,

Yet nothing that really needs saying,
You already know.

Forgive the tears... they are only bits
of selfishness that can be contained no longer.
I only wish to keep you a little longer,
Within the boundaries of my immediate life.

And so thank you for
touching my life
For letting me know you
And love you...

Author Unknown

Thinking about the prose was making me feel very melancholy. I tried to keep a stiff upper lip but a deluge of emotion tied to pieces of memories burned past my brain. I realized in that moment that it all was changing. I tried to tell myself, it's just a move Jane, you have done this so many times before, but that's not how I felt.

Why are you having such a difficult time now, I wondered? But there was no answer, just an empty void. I hugged many close friends and acquaintances. Finally it was over and we stood alone with each other after saying all our final farewells.

We knew we had to hurry home as we had so much to do yet and the evening was late. The packers would be loading up the house the next day! My brain kicked in, I grabbed Gary's hand, stood on my tip toes and whispered in his ear, "I'll follow you anywhere, I love you." He smiled, and I smiled too. A chapter in my life had ended, but another was just starting and we were ready, as ready as we could be, having crammed so much into such a small window of time.

Moving

The final day in our home came, the packers had loaded up the moving van and it was on its way to Springfield. We were exhausted, both physically and emotionally. We stood out front, looking at our home of two years with such an overwhelming feeling. What an amazing two years it had been. It had been a very successful two years for Gary with having a very prestigious command. It had been a joy to live near our daughter Elizabeth, son-in-law James and JT. I would miss that little guy so much; it was too painful to even imagine what it would be like not being close by to him and sharing day to day life. I couldn't bring myself to have them there when we moved out. I knew it would be hard just leaving, but to have Elizabeth, James and JT there would have put me over the edge! Memories were flooding back on the days after 9/11 and what we all had to deal with while living at Fort Bragg and then my decision to go and help. How could I leave this place, a place that had watched me grow and challenge myself, a place that had recognized me as being someone special, their 'hometown hero'. I knew it would all change once I moved. Hardly anyone knew me in the DC area, and I was going there to be a 'nobody' and not the 'somebody' I was at Fort Bragg.

Our neighbor and friend, Diane, was leaving the same day also. Her husband, Bill, was already at his new job, freshly retired from the military. They were such great friends and had made our stay at Fort Bragg so enjoyable. We were all pretty inseparable during those two years. When I say the Army is small, it is so true. Diane and Bill, Gary and I had been friends for years with all of us being at different Army posts at the same time. We knew we would be friends forever and little did we know that we would continue in the future living near each other.

Diane walked down to our house and threw her arms around us both. "Here we go again," she said. "It's hard realizing Bill's military career is over and he's starting off in the civilian world after all these years! I will miss you guys so much. Bill is sad too that he couldn't be here to say goodbye." "I've got a bottle of champagne," she exclaimed, "to celebrate our departure, do you have any glasses or is everything gone?"

"I do have some plastic glasses for the road trip," I said.

Diane handed the bottle to Gary and he did the honors of opening it. He poured the champagne into our glasses and we all became very quiet. We had all been through so much together and this chapter was closing. We looked at each other as we always did when we toasted, right into each other's eyes and said our traditional toast, "it's FRIDAY!!!!" (The toast would change depending on the day of the week!)

"Okay, we have to commemorate this day with a picture and I just happen to have my camera right here, so let's set the timer and put it on the top of the car and we can stand in front of our house and get a final picture of us," I said.

It seemed so appropriate for us all to drive off at the same time and that is just what we did. We let Diane drive away first and then we followed right behind. We drove through the post for the last time and as we left the Army gate, Diane drove straight and we turned off to the right honking our horns as we all departed.

Farewell Fort Bragg… what is in store for us in Virginia?

CHAPTER 22

Settling in and saying goodbye

It would be an understatement to say *I'm overwhelmed* when you move to a new location. Every two years or so, to pick up and say goodbye to all of your friends, colleagues, acquaintances, not to mention your hairdresser, doctor and dentist! The list goes on and on and the military spouse repeatedly does this so many times throughout their spouse's military career.

The movers kept unloading the plethora of boxes and furniture. *Where would it all go*? I thought. I say it every time and somehow, everything finds its place. This move was a particularly difficult one as I knew that not moving to a military post would have its challenges. My neighborhood friends would, most likely, not be associated with the military. I had been told to be prepared, neighborhoods in the Washington, DC area were said to be on the unfriendly side. Most homeowners just kept to themselves, one could go an entire lifetime and not know who their neighbor was! That would need to be remedied, but in due time.

I had been preparing for this and had made a plan. I decided before I left Fort Bragg, I needed to expand my horizons; do something for me, something that would be rewarding. I felt the need to 'give back' and in a big way. I contacted USA Freedom Corps, the organization that President Bush talked about when I had the amazing luck of meeting him in March. I found out that there was a program within USA Freedom Corps entitled Medical Reserve Corps (MRC). Wow, this seemed to be right up my alley! I was told that their goals were to provide the structure necessary to deploy medical and public health personnel in response to an emergency, and as luck would have it, it was just becoming a reality. When we traveled to Virginia in the springtime, in search of our home, I met with Mary, a Public Health Nurse, who was the coordinator of the MRC. She was quite eager to get me involved and we made a plan that once I felt settled enough in my new home in Springfield, I would begin to volunteer with her and the MRC.

The dogs frolicked in their fenced in back yard while Gary and I struggled to get the house in order, well some semblance of order, I should say. We were pushing to get everything unpacked as quickly as we could so I could begin on my new volunteer journey and Gary could begin his new military assignment.

I was delighted that I had a volunteer project I could sink my teeth into. I wanted to feel part of something much bigger and USA Freedom Corps was just what I needed. It was located in the White House complex in a lovely little brownstone located on Jackson Place. I was told that I would have my own desk and a computer during the days I was volunteering. *Pinch me! Could this be real?* I had my own space at the White House?

Mary had me involved from the get go and I just loved it. USA Freedom Corps was such a new concept and was at the grass roots level, so there was a significant amount of planning and organizing that had to be done. I attended the Freedom Corps meetings with Mary and was made to feel like part of the team. Because MRC also fell under the Office of the Surgeon General, at the Department of Health and Human Services, half my time was spent volunteering in Bethesda.

Volunteering had its perks as I could determine which hours I wanted to work. This became an opportunity for my mother and me to continue the close relationship we had finally developed. Who knew how much time I would have left with her? The doctor had said two years or less. She lived only a short two hours away in Chester, Virginia. My weekly visits became a cherished time for both of us. Mostly we would sit and talk and reminisce, remembering only the happy times. Oh my, was my mother a changed woman, no more of the negativity that seemed to surround her before her hospitalization!

Beauty day ensued whenever I visited. It seemed that I was the only one she felt comfortable with styling her hair. She would wash her hair before I arrived and then I would cut it and curl it for her, her head full of wire bristle curlers. It was a small thing that I could do, but it became our special time. Farewells were always bitter sweet. She would walk me to her front door and tell me she loved me, hug me and say, "Hurry back I will really miss you." My heart smiled!

I eventually realized that the commute to my volunteer job was becoming overwhelming; as many do that live in the DC area. Not only was it getting expensive, it was a huge time commitment just in the commute alone. The days that I worked at the White House, I would take the metro and when I worked at HHS, I would drive. Traffic was a nightmare and the commute was freakishly long. As much as I enjoyed the work that I was doing, I knew that it was time to consider getting a job where I could receive an income. Seven months after beginning my volunteer job, I informed Mary that it was time for me to consider a paying job.

The only place that held an interest to me was working for a nonprofit organization. I perused the employment section of the Washington Post and the internet hoping I would find something. As luck would have it, there was a position available. One month later, I became the Health Coordinator for their program, a very large job!

Unfortunately this put a halt to my weekday visits to my mother. She and I were saddened by this turn of events. I still visited, but now on the weekends with Gary. It wasn't quite the same but it would have to do.

How do I know I'm seeing you for the last time?

"Jane, you have a phone call," interrupted Debbie, during a planning meeting in mid June. "Someone has been calling and calling, it must be important!"

"Thanks Deb, I'll go and see. Sorry everyone, I'll be right back," I said as I hurriedly left the meeting room.

"Mom, Dad has been calling and calling you. Where have you been?" Elizabeth said into the phone.

"Honey, I always have a meeting at 9:00 in the morning. I don't have time to talk! What's going on?"

"Oh, I don't want to be the one to tell you Mom! Grandma died this morning. We have been on the phone with Melissa. She really wants to talk to you, she is pretty upset. Mom…. Are you there?" she asked.

"Oh my god, what happened?" I asked, stunned. A group of office mates moved closer to comfort me.

"Dad is on his way to pick you up, and he will fill you in. I'm sorry I had to be the one to tell you. Oh Mom, she's gone! I can't believe it!" she wailed.

I slowly hung up the phone and mouthed the words, "My mother died this morning!" I could barely stand up. Debi grabbed a chair and gently guided me down.

"Oh sweetie, I'm so sorry. What can I do for you? Can I get you anything, call anyone?" she offered.

I sat there staring blankly into space, "I guess I need to find out where Gary is. I just need to go home; I need to figure this out!"

With the help of my office mates, they walked me down

the stairs to the main entrance of the building. Gary was there waiting. As he reached his arms out to me when I ran to meet him, I noticed that he had visibly been crying. "I'm so sorry, Jane. I mean you were just beginning to have this great relationship with her! It's not fair!" he said, burying his head into my neck.

I left my car in the parking lot, sometime, someday I would go and pick it up, and it was the least of my worries. I needed to get home; I needed to talk to my sister.

"I had a feeling something wasn't right, Janie," Melissa cried into the phone. "I spent the night at her house last night, I never do that! But I felt unsettled. I had to work today so I wanted to make sure that she had used the bathroom before I left, so I helped her in. Janie, as we were walking in, she looked at me and said 'I love you' and then as she sat down she kind of looked funny and said 'I feel dizzy'. She just laid her head on my chest and stopped breathing. That was it! She was gone!"

My throat was closing in on me and I could barely get a word out, I was so choked up with emotion. "I know Mom wants to be cremated, but I need to see her one last time. Can I come down this afternoon? I need to see you too Melissa. I'm so sorry; I can't imagine how frightening of an experience it was for you! But I am so glad that you were there with her, I'm so glad that you spent the night. Oh, thank you so much!"

"She is at a funeral home now and won't be cremated until the morning. I would love it if you would come down today. I'll meet you at the funeral home. You know, we have so many plans to work on Janie and I need your help, okay? We will have to have the funeral in Ohio so she can be buried next to Dad and Scott."

Melissa was waiting for me in the lobby as I arrived at the

212

funeral home. We held each other for an eternity it seemed. "Have you talked to Martin?" I asked

"He is really pretty shaken. He and BL will meet us in Ohio. I told him that we would let him know as soon as we made arrangements with the funeral home in Ohio," she said grabbing my hand. "They are expecting you; they know that you want to see Mom. I can't see her right now. I'm an emotional heap, is that okay?"

"Of course it is okay. You have been through hell and back today and I promise I will only be gone for a few minutes, take a seat, look at a magazine and I will be back before you know it," I said trying to act so strong. I had no clue if I could do this on my own and see my mother for the last time.

"Can I ask you a question," I asked the gentleman that was taking me to see Mom. "It might be an unusual request, I don't know, but do you have any scissors? I'd like to take a lock of my mother's hair. Is that possible?"

"Oh yes, you are not the first one to have asked for that. I will get the scissors and bring you an envelope so you can have a safe place for it," he smiled.

I have that envelope, and it has never been opened. I hold a small piece of her, the part that became our bond, and the part that in its own way brought our relationship full circle.

CHAPTER 23

Ben

It was Monday morning, very early and I was sitting outside the HR office trying to make sense of what had transpired within the last few weeks of my life. I felt a chill run through me, the kind of cold that you feel clear down to your bones but that cannot easily be remedied. What had happened to my life?

Here I had just gone through one of those most hellacious moments in my entire adult life and was now listening to Valerie, the Human Resources director tell me that the nightmare I'd hoped I had concluded by drawing it out into the light was like a grenade that had exploded on my personal life, making my problems visible to all. Saying I was not happy was an understatement. Whatever happened to employee support? Sexual harassment was supposed to be against the law and something that *would not be tolerated*, or so the company policy stated, but what happened to carrying out that policy? How had this gotten so *big*?

An hour passed before signs of life began to dawn in the building. I could hear the familiar hustle and bustle of people coming to work, getting coffee, and getting settled in. I could also hear the constant flutter of phones coming to life.

I looked up just as Valerie rounded the corner. She looked surprised and confused as she opened her office door.

"Jane, have you been waiting long?" she asked. I stood up and stretched.

"Not long but this can't wait," I told her.

"What's wrong?" she asked but when we exchanged looks, she didn't ask again. And from the look on her face I could see that the subject she knew I was there for was not one she liked discussing. I followed her in and took a seat across from her. She folded her hands on her desk and took a breath. This was not good.

"I'm sorry Jane; I know this has got to be tough for you. Unfortunately for now, you will have to continue to work with him," she explained.

My mind was reeling. Did she just say I had to *continue* working with him? Would they expect a rape victim to continue working with her rapist? What was going on here?

"That's it? That's the solution? Wait it out? Just endure the second degree of hell while you guys figure out what to do?" I was fuming. Valerie looked uncomfortable like a naughty child that had been caught stealing and was now paying the consequences. Obviously she'd hadn't expected me to react, and certainly not in that way. I guess she just assumed I was going to roll over and take it. But I'd had enough of taking it.

I stood outside her office and collected myself before heading back. I could still hear him going off on me... I closed my eyes as the memory surfaced, feeling as fresh as the day it had happened.

An employee had come to my office distraught. I told him to come in and sit down and we could talk and then closed the door.

Almost immediately the phone rang, but when I saw it was my boss, I didn't answer because it would have been rude to interrupt the employee who was pouring his heart out to me about a work issue. I talked to the guy for about 45 minutes which seemed to help.

By the time he left, he was feeling much more in control of himself. I walked him down the hall afterwards and saw my boss coming down to meet me. It was apparent from the scowl on his face and the way he was walking towards me, that he wasn't happy.

"Jane, when I call, you will answer the phone! I had something very important to discuss with you," he growled.

I tried to inform him about the situation I'd been dealing with but he insisted that I drop everything I was doing anytime he wanted to talk to me. I was shocked, not only was that unprofessional, but it was against my own ethics. I was here to help people, not placate his ego. So I told him that there was no way I was going to do that as that was part of my job to assist the employees on health issues, physically or mentally. Ben became incensed.

"You will let me know the next time you are in your office and refuse to answer your phone!" he screamed in a huff then stormed off.

"What did you need to tell me that was so important?" I asked.

"Never mind! It's too late now, and it doesn't matter!" he yelled down the hall.

I opened my eyes and I walked back to my office with a feeling of dread. I just knew deep down that this could never turn out well. It was as if I had predicted the future.

The only good thing about the day was that Ben kept his distance from me for the entire next day. In some ways it was a relief, but in others it was a feeling of impending doom. *What was he thinking, what was he planning?* I knew that I wasn't off the hook; the reprieve was only temporary, as he would still find ways to make my life miserable.

I felt I knew why his anger was so intense, why he felt he had to lash back at me. It was not that I understood it, or accepted it; it was just how he was. The previous week, I had turned down his advances. It was ever so subtle; he called me into his office and closing the door, stood right next to me and asked me if I would like to go to New York City with him and visit the Ground Zero site for a weekend. I was

218

totally taken aback, and became quite uncomfortable. I just didn't know what to say! I hemmed and hawed and said, "Well, I don't know, I need to discuss it with Gary, and if I did go, it couldn't be for overnight."

I went back to my office and felt sick to my stomach, thinking that our friendship had gone too far. Now what? I called my husband and discussed it with him. He said, "Jane you have to document everything that is being said from now on, okay? This is sexual harassment and you also need to go talk to Human Resources." I sat down at my computer and wrote down what had taken place that day and then saved the file on my thumb drive so I could take it home.

I didn't go up to HR right away as I needed time to think about it and discuss it in more detail with Gary. After going home and becoming quite emotional about it and feeling that I must have done something to lead him on, Gary looked at me and said, "This is a normal reaction for someone going through this, you have been really taken advantage of and you don't deserve this!" The military really has done a lot of training in this area and he knew just what I needed to do.

"But what if I am wrong and this is nothing?" I asked.

"This is obviously something; Ben is just doing this so gradually to make it look like nothing. Did anyone else hear this conversation about New York?" he asked. I shook my head. "No, of course not, as he knows what he is doing. He doesn't want anyone else to know that he has done this, which is why he closed the door! You really need to tell him first of all that you were uncomfortable with his offer and then you need to go to HR," Gary explained.

"Talk about feeling uncomfortable, I will really be if I have to say that to him!" I exclaimed. "Oh, I just can't imagine saying that."

"Believe me, Jane, you have to, I know that it is hard and

I don't envy you having the conversation. I'm trying to be rational about this but I want to kick his ass!" he exclaimed.

A hint of a smile came over me in the midst of all of my anguish. Somehow it was nice to know that my husband was willing to fight for me! He was giving me the strength to do this, even if it was just a pep talk, it helped. I was feeling so vulnerable and hearing Gary's words really helped focus me. I knew I could go in the next day and face my demons.

I got to work early, as I often do. I'm such a morning person, but today I was really tired, as I still didn't sleep well the night before, worrying on how to handle it correctly. I decided to drive to work by myself, instead of taking my car pool. Ben was already at work when I arrived. I was mentally preparing what to say and was hoping he would give me a few minutes to get some coffee and settle in. He must have heard me unlock my door as he immediately walked down to my office and stood in the doorway smiling. I looked up at him from behind my desk, and took a deep breath and waited. "Hi Jane, I hope you had a good evening yesterday. Did you, by any chance, give my question about New York some more thought?" Ben asked.

"Ben, I must be honest with you. Your offer made me very uncomfortable. I'm happily married and so taking a trip to New York is something I just cannot do," I blurted.

Ben's whole demeanor changed right in front of me. He went from smiling to a look of disgust/anger and snapped. "I thought you would say that." With that he stormed out of my office and slammed his office door behind him.

I was shaking. I still had an hour before I could go up to HR and talk to them, as it was so early. In the meantime, I shut my door to my office, closed my eyes and breathed deeply several times, trying to regain my composure. I knew it would be difficult but didn't quite think that. *Don't start*

220

crying now Jane, don't let him win! I kept saying over and over to myself.

I decided the best thing to do was to take a walk and get away from the area for a while. Our office area was secluded at the end of the hall and with the other nurse not at work yet for the day, I didn't want to be in the same area alone with him. He seemed pretty angry and I didn't want to take any chances!

I went to the cafeteria and got some coffee and just sat there trying to compose myself prior to going to talk to HR. My friend, Marilyn, came in to get some coffee and walked up to me and said, "Who died, Jane?"

"Marilyn, I would love to talk to you about it, but right now I just can't. I am dealing with a bit of an office problem and I'm trying to figure out the best way to handle it," I said.

"Well, just so you know, I'm here if you need to talk," she said.

I went upstairs to the 8th floor to talk to my HR representative, Valerie. "Hi Valerie, do you have a few minutes to give me, I need to discuss an issue with you privately," I said.

Valerie said, "Jane, is everything okay? You look a bit distraught."

Oh great, my face is an open book, everyone can tell how I am feeling. As hard as I have always tried to hide my emotions, it's never worked. I quietly said, "Well, it's confidential, and I am a bit distraught."

She immediately got up and said, "Follow me; I know where we can talk privately." I was relieved that I wouldn't have to discuss this while she was sitting in her cube. She found a nice private empty office.

"Oh Valerie, I have to report something and this is very

difficult for me to do," I blurted. "Ben is just a bit too friendly. I noticed it before and I tried to ignore it, but now…" I trailed off as tears were beginning to flow. I tried so hard to fight back the tears and be strong, but I couldn't.

"What happened?" she exclaimed.

I blew my nose, regained what composure I could regain and said, "Yesterday, he asked me to go away with him for the weekend to New York. He knows that I am married, happily."

"Did you confront him about it?" she asked.

"I didn't yesterday, but did this morning and told him how uncomfortable it made me feel. He got defensive and angry and went to his office," I said.

"Well, you did the right thing, Jane. I want you to document what happened, as will I in your records. I will discuss this with my boss and see what our next step is. Unfortunately for now, you will have to continue to work with him," she explained.

As fate would have it, it happened later that week just after HR talked to him. During which time he flatly denied everything I'd told them. No surprise there, he was acting just as I expected him to, arrogant and cutting. I ran into him in the hall as I was making my rounds. His disdain shined in his eyes like fireflies in summer. At that moment I was sure he hated me. But I didn't care, I just wanted all of this to go away and be behind me.

"Well Jane, thanks to you, I have to go through some sort of HR training because you think you are being harassed! I will just have to see when I can fit this training in to my busy schedule as I have so much to do and you apparently have all the time in the world to just wander the halls and talk to everyone, making up stories, telling lies. Now they tell me that when we have our daily meeting, it will have to be with the door open because poor little ol' you feels uncomfortable around big ol' meanie me!" he scoffed.

There were so many things I wanted to say, so much I could have said. But what would be the point? I knew that it would only fuel the fire and make my job more of a living hell than it already was. It was tough enough as it was, so I kept quiet and said nothing. Nothing I could do or say was going to make a difference.

Every day was terrible. Frequently I'd go to work with my stomach in knots. It got so bad that I dreaded going in which was sad because then I hated that feeling as I loved where I was working. I loved the work and helping people. But dealing with Ben was making life unbearable. I half heartedly started perusing web sites looking for other jobs. As much as I loved the organization I worked for, no job was worth this amount of abuse.

But what I couldn't figure out was why he was always so angry and such a self centered man? It made me wonder what had happened to him along the way that had made him turn out the way he had? Once he'd told me that he was married but his wife did not want to move to the DC area, so she stayed behind on the west coast. It didn't make sense to me. Obviously there were problems but that was their business. Still it made me wonder if that factored into any of this.

He had a particularly annoying habit of bragging about himself as if he were superior to anyone else, this arrogance spilled over to include both men and women. He was always going on and on about how he used to be a body builder and that sometime I should see some of his pictures. No matter how many times I tried to politely dissuade him, he still couldn't tell I had no interest.

In fact, he did show these photos to me. I tried to

downplay everything, thinking that it reinforced what I believed to be true that he was actually a very insecure man, needing to build himself up all the time was the only way he could make himself feel better. How truly pathetic he was and he didn't even know it.

Even though I could see that he had these problems, there was nothing that I could do. I was helpless and being helpless is such a demeaning feeling. It was like a sore that continue to grow and fester with each new day, each assaulting incident.

Every day without fail there would be some new negativity that he would throw my way. He never tired of the routine. And on the flip side I just did my best to ignore it, ignore dealing with the abuse. But at the same time I was writing it all down and saving and storing information on every bit of it. I felt I needed to have everything backed up, just in case.

Then one afternoon he caught up with me just as I was coming back from lunch. In his eyes there was pure hatred, such vile contempt for me and I'd done nothing, nothing to earn it but just be a good employee. I so desperately wanted to be anywhere else but I had no choice, I either accepted defeat and quit or stood my ground. Abruptly he stopped in front of me so I took a breath trying to prepare myself for the onslaught I knew would follow.

"Oh Jane, you need to stop driving with your car pool. I need to have you coming in earlier and have no idea when we will be finished each day. You should also not plan your 'lunch dates' with your friends as there will be many days you will need to work through lunch," he told me with a glint in his eyes. It was clear that he felt like he was victorious. But I refused to let him win. And I refused to succumb to cowardice.

"Ben, I deserve to go to lunch like anyone else and will

continue to do so," I told him. "If there are certain days that you need me to work, please let me know in advance. The same thing goes with my carpool," I added, then I started to walk away.

"Must be nice, but since I have more education than you and have the job as manager, which you could never do, I have to work the longer hours. But don't worry, I will let you know when I need you early or late or during lunch, so don't get too comfortable," he squawked and stormed off. He had obviously expected me to surrender.

But the days just continued to get bleaker. On one September day in 2004, the contract nurse that was working with me and Ben informed us that she would be leaving. My heart just sank. I knew what that meant. That meant, until they hired someone new, I would be in the office complex at the end of the hall, with *just* Ben. I just could not imagine being left alone down there with just him. It made me feel ill just thinking about it.

That prompted me to march back to HR. I was shaking and visibly worried as I explained to Valerie how uncomfortable that this new reality would be for me.

"I totally get it," she assured squeezing my hand. I swallowed back the tears and the lump in my throat. She had no idea, nor would anyone who had never gone through it, how awful it really was. "Let me see if I can get a hold of Ben's boss, maybe talking to her would help," she offered. But in my mind, I could only see things getting worse. She was about to unleash a hive of angry hornets

As a result I began calling weekly, just to check on the status. I was trying not to let my fears consume me but my fears were so overwhelming. I even offered to move up to a different floor during that time.

But in the end, nothing was done which wounded me

introspectively a lot. I was beginning to feel like I was becoming a pest to HR. As if that wasn't bad enough, I found I was also being ignored.

And through the heart of all this old mister mean mouth would still make his caustic comments whenever he could. Every time he'd see me, he had to say something, like: "You would get more work done Jane if you weren't always running to HR and complaining like a school girl."

It was very clear I was alone and on my own. No one wanted to support me, even though they all knew how Ben was. Worse, many had personally witnessed his outrageous behavior and heard his snide and often cruel remarks towards me and still, turned a blind eye. No one wanted to understand how uncomfortable this all was. No one wanted to get involved or to counter him. Essentially I was left with the choice: Suck it up and deal with it or quit.

I started going for job interviews, but my heart wasn't really in it. I was hoping that might help somehow. The irony was, I really did believe in the organization. If only they'd showed me the same kind of loyalty. But being loyal didn't get me anywhere. I should have gone with my gut and pursued another job.

Eventually in November the job was filled by another nurse. I was delighted to have someone in the office next to me. Bev was very pleasant and so easy to talk to. It was wonderful to feel relieved again, so much so that I let my guard down and eventually told her why I was so pleased that she was there in the office next to me. I touched lightly on Ben's verbal abuse and my concern for being alone in the office with him. Initially she appeared to be so sympathetic to what I said. Little did I know that I should have kept my mouth shut as my words given in confidence would only come back to haunt me.

As it turned out in early January the HR group that our department fell under was planning to take a day trip, to celebrate the holidays. We were going to Union Station for the day and were going to go to a movie. I had it planned that I would drive our office mates to the event. Then at about 11:00 o'clock I walked to Bev's office and said, 'So, are we still all set to drive to Union Station together?'

"Oh, didn't Julie tell you yesterday?" she said. "We decided to walk to the event together as it is such a nice day." I was a little surprised but I thought: No big deal. It wasn't until she added the next comment that I felt the knife go in and twist in my gut. She was no friend.

"But you can still take Ben with you," she quipped almost laughing. I was flabbergasted and so hurt. She knew how uncomfortable that I felt being alone with him, and now I would have to drive him to this event? No way!

I decided not to go at the last minute and thankfully Ben found someone else to give him a ride. I just felt so uncomfortable with the whole situation that staying behind seemed to make more sense to me. I ended up having a very busy day at the office and felt glad that I made the decision to stay. Working was just what I needed to be doing.

Unfortunately, if work was a blessing that day, the next day was just the opposite and wound up being one of the worst days of my entire life. To start, Bev totally ignored talking to me when she came in. I guess I understood, since I didn't go to the event.

"Jane, we are having a meeting at 9:00 in Ben's office," she stoically stated.

"Okay," I said with a half smile. "Is everything okay?" Then out of blue came the bombshell.

"Don't talk to me Jane, we will discuss it at the meeting!" she yelled.

Discuss what? My brain was numb. I couldn't understand her bizarre behavior. But all the same, at 9:00 I walked down to Ben's office for the meeting feeling overwhelmed with dread. I just knew that this was not going to turn out well. I could feel it deep in my gut.

I walked in to see Ben sitting behind his desk and Bev with Julie. Julie closed the door. No one spoke for a while and then Julie spoke.

"Jane, what the heck is wrong? You have become so quiet, you are so sad. We just don't understand," she said.

"When you didn't show up at the event yesterday, I had to make excuses for you, and that was really uncomfortable, why didn't you show up?" Bev asked.

They waited like vultures for carrion but I said nothing. I was being confronted in a room of my peers with no HR support to be by my side. How was this fair? But it became very clear to me that this was just what Ben had wanted and obviously orchestrated with the intent on humiliating me. Ben continued to say nothing, but had a smirk on his face that said it all. I was caught in a lion's lair and had no way of getting out. I held my head down fighting tears. *Damn them, how dare they confront me like this in front of my boss*!

"You do your work very well Jane," Ben said. "But it is more than work that you need to do, you need to be part of the group, you need to discuss what is going on with us. When you shut down at work, it affects everything," he said smugly.

"I can't do this! I don't want to say why I didn't go yesterday, please do not make me say this, not here, not now," I stammered struggling not to break down.

"Jane, you can't go on like this, you have to talk to us," Bev chimed in, in a very hostile voice. "I thought you were my friend Jane, and then you get all quiet and it affects me when you do that." I was beside myself. Was she for real? It was unbelievable. I knew she knew exactly how awful all of this had been for me and for her to be so cruel, it was almost worse than Ben's inappropriate overtures.

"I couldn't go yesterday as I felt uncomfortable being alone with Ben," I blurted. This has been happening for some time. When you women decided not to drive with me, I knew I would be left going with just him, and I couldn't do it," I said as evenly as I could without tears, without raising my voice. I was determined he wasn't going to win.

I didn't wait for their remarks instead I immediately picked up my papers and walked out of the room then literally ran to my office and closed the door. On autopilot I got on my computer and quickly wrote a letter of resignation, hit the printed function then got up and abruptly walked out of my office.

"What the hell are you so upset about?" Ben yelled at me as I headed for the elevator. "Jane, come back here! We are not yet finished with this conversation!" he shrieked.

But I refused to turn around. I refused to give him that satisfaction. I'd had enough, enough of him, enough of them, enough of Bev and the whole place that hadn't done right by me. I was just too hurt and too upset. I walked up to HR and of course Valerie was not there. I saw her boss, Janet, and told her that I need to talk to her *right now*. Janet saw how very upset I was and walked me to her office and closed the door. It all came spilling out, the floodgate had been opened. Ben and Bev had committed their last atrocity.

"Janet, I can't deal with any of this anymore. I am hurt beyond belief and too upset to remain here any longer. Here is my letter of resignation," I told her setting it on her desk.

"Jane, don't do that... there is no reason for this, please! I won't accept this. I'll tell you what, go home, and I will do some research on all of this and call you later, okay?" Janet pleaded.

"Okay, but I will have to take a taxi, as I drove with my car pool today," I sniffed.

"No problem, why don't you wait a few minutes before you go get your purse? So we make sure that Ben isn't there, okay?" she suggested.

Luckily I was able to sneak into my office about fifteen minutes later and retrieve my belongings. I looked back at my office on the way out and realized that this was probably the last day I would be there.

I cried the whole way home. I cried when I talked to Gary on the phone. I wanted to crawl in a hole and die. My stomach was a wreck, I felt like I would throw up. Over and over again, I just kept thinking: What the heck happened? How did this go so wrong?

The following day at 4:00 in the afternoon, the phone rang and it was Valerie. I could tell even before she told me that the news wasn't going to be good.

"Jane, we have reviewed what happened today and we have decided that yesterday was your last day working with us, we accept your resignation."

"Wait," I said, "You don't have my resignation, Janet handed it back it me".

"Jane, yesterday *was* your last day. What day do you want to come in and pick up your belongings in your office? You will need an escort and your husband cannot come in to the building with you," Valerie said, as if she were some sort of robot! The supportive woman I had initially talked to was gone. She was all business, removed and detached. Apparently Ben's squad had gotten to her as well or she was afraid to take a stand, in any event, it was obvious that I was on the short end of the stick and I was going to stay there no matter what I did.

Everything I had thought of her and the organization up to that point came tumbling down. I hadn't expected her to be a friend, but I had expected she would at least be fair and do her job, but now she had revealed her true colors and she was neither. I felt so be betrayed.

"Thank you, I will be in on Saturday to pick my stuff up." Then I quietly said "Goodbye".

They had made me feel as if I were a criminal. As if I were to blame when I knew I didn't do anything wrong! I just could not understand what was happening. How Ben could be allowed to get away with this and worse while the rest of the staff and the organization were going along with it. This was a company known for their supposed un-biasness and fairness. Well, they'd just fallen off their proverbial pedestal. It just happened so fast… in a blink of an eye, the organization I had loved and respected so much was telling me not to return. Where was their loyalty to me?

After all of that falderal I went into a deep depression that I could not see a way out of it. Fortunately for me though I was surrounded by family and loved ones who cared. And one of those people, my son Ian's girlfriend, Jenny, who had just moved from Georgia to be near Ian, helped ne find a good therapist. Each week she took me to my appointment and patiently waited in the car, giving me space. Little by little, I could see it was helping. I was starting to get my old "me" back.

Jenny was my saving grace. She was so easy to talk to and seemed to really understand. I found the therapist intimidating and my sessions painful as I had to talk about Ben, that in turn made me think of him, something I didn't want to do. But it was helping me to dispel the strength of his hold on me.

231

Eventually I went on anti-depressants and slowly I started to rally. From there I sought a lawyer and Gary and I went to see him together to see if there was anything that could be done about the despicable way I had been treated. After many weeks of meeting with him, the consensus came down that it would be an uphill battle that likely we'd lose. Great! So Ben and his entourage had gotten away with it.

And the company and job I had loved so much became a part of my dark past. I would never again work for them or sing their praises (as I had before) or referrals. I might not have exposed them for what they had done, but damage had been done.

After that, I applied for many jobs and was offered several. I eventually settled on something fun, as that is what I thought I needed to be doing then. Here I am, five years later doing that very fun job, managing the Travelers Clinic at George Washington University in their clinic building, Medical Faculty Associates. I now have a boss that treats me fairly and maturely, and I couldn't ask for more. I love my patients and love the staff. So I guess it's true, when one door closes, another opens. And this door is definitely the better of the two. At last I am proud of my work again, and more precious than that, I am happy and eager to go to work.

The damage I had sustained and endured while with the other organization was unbelievable. Ben and the terrible lack of support from the other organization had nearly ruined that for me. When I think of all the times he had literally ripped off my reports and micro managed me to his advantage, then turned around and treated me so abominably, it amazes me that I stayed as long as I did and endured so much. But those terrible days are behind me. And thank God that the faith I have in myself and humanity has now been restored. Thank God for second chances and new beginnings.

CHAPTER 24

Shaky Ground

One September Friday evening in 2006, after Gary and I had gotten home from work, we settled down for dinner. I'd just thrown a simple menu together of pasta and salad as I was tired. But because I was tired and had had a particularly frustrating day I had poured us both a glass of wine and was eager to share the details of my day with him.

Of course I knew it was tenuous at best that he would share because Gary had not been reciprocating details about his days, feelings or anything else for quite some time now. But I was bound and determined to make this work between us and just as stubborn to penetrate his armor.

When we were finally seated I noticed his reluctance to start his meal, it made me confused. Was he not in the mood for pasta? Did he not feel well? In the thirty years we'd been married, Gary has never once complained, nor refused to eat something I made.

"Is something wrong?" I asked watching him push and poke his pasta with his fork.

"No. Nothing," he said quietly then seemed almost to drift off again. I swallowed trying to quell my frustration.

I watched him pick up his spoon to twirl his spaghetti, as he always did. He promptly put the spoon down and picked up his fork and let out a long sigh.

"Gary?" He just looked at me. "What's going on?"

"Nothing," he quipped and kept on eating. I could feel the fury burning within me. What was he keeping from me? Why would he just answer so abruptly?

"If you tell me "nothing" one more time..." I spit between gritted teeth. "I swear I'm going to lose it. Now what the hell is going on?" I pressed. And for the first time I saw a great sadness come into his eyes. That look scared me. For a fleeting second I feared he was going to reveal something really awful like: he was having an affair or was going to divorce me. For the first time I felt very alone and wondered if we really would make it.

As quickly as that look came across his face it was gone. As if nothing ever happened he looked very calmly at me and said, "Jane, there is nothing wrong, I just have a lot on my mind lately."

Well at least he said something, I thought. As per my usual pattern, I tried to encourage him to talk about it and said, "What's going on with work? Is it a specifically stressful time right now?"

"It's always stressful and I don't know what I want to do when I get out, stay with the same job or look for another," he said, as he was slowly trying to twirl the spaghetti on his fork.

I knew that this was such a huge turning point in his life, transitioning out of the military and not knowing where his career was headed. He didn't get picked up on the new list of one star general and I know that was part of his sadness. He was such a great military officer and I know it had to be a painful time for him. Though for me, it was just conjecture as he simply refused to discuss it. In fact he pretty much refused to discuss most of his life with me.

I decided to change the subject and I know I should have been more careful with my words and say something sweet and cheery, but no, I had to make a dig, "Why don't you use your spoon to twirl the spaghetti like you always do?" I asked. Little did I know that this was a sign that I wished I had not noticed.

"Jane, just let me do it how I want to and stop nagging me," he said a bit louder than I deserved.

"Excuse me? I was just trying to carry on some sort of

conversation with you," I said. "I don't need to feel attacked. God, you are so quiet, it's like pulling teeth to get you to say anything."

"Just don't criticize me about how I eat, okay?" He asked.

"I'm sorry, I shouldn't have said anything," I stammered as my eyes started welling up with tears.

I was feeling a dull ache in my stomach that wasn't going away so I gathered my plate up, still full of food and tossed the contents into the trash. "I lost my appetite," I said. "I think I will go upstairs and read a book for a while.

I went up to our room feeling hopeless. It was a typical night, little communication with each other and it left me so frustrated. I refused to sit up in our room and cry all night, so I opened my book and started to read, but I just couldn't focus on the words, my mind kept thinking about Gary's and my life together.

Was I just being selfish, wanting him to share in all that was going on? I wish I had someone to talk to about it, but there wasn't anyone I felt that I could confide in except my sister and she didn't need to be hearing all of that. I tried to rationalize my behavior and realized that it was wrong of me to confront him about how he was eating. But God, I didn't need to be jumped for such a little thing! Gary was hurting and I needed to find out what the hell was going on.

If he decided that he wouldn't talk to me about what was going on, I needed to give him an ultimatum I thought. I just can't deal with this limbo anymore! What could we do to get our marriage back on track? I needed to let him know that this time I was serious; this non-communication was just not working for me anymore! How could he think that everything was okay and why did I have to put up with the same stuff day after day?

What could I do to make him understand that I was serious

this time about it? I deserved better! I would talk to him more about it in the morning I decided.

Around midnight I heard the door creak open and Gary quietly enter. He undressed in the bathroom and then tiptoed into the bedroom and turned back the covers on his side of the bed and got in. I pretended to be asleep. Now wasn't a time for conversation, as I knew it would just upset me and then I would never sleep… I would wait until morning.

Sleep was fitful but I did sleep. At least he was next to me.

Saturday morning came with sunlight streaming in the window. It was just a beautiful day. The window was slightly opened and I could hear the birds chirping and felt a bit of briskness to the air. I thought *this seems like a perfect day*! I got up letting Gary get a bit more sleep and called quietly for our dog, Womack, to come join me and we both scrambled down the stairs. *Ah, there is nothing like a beautiful day to put your life into perspective* I thought. Little did I realize that this day would be a turning point in my life.

I blindly went through the morning motions, feed the dog, and get the coffee. I was on autopilot. I grabbed my coffee in one hand and the newspaper in the other deciding that what I really needed was to enjoy the sun. Mack and I strolled to the sun-room and I opened the back door to let him outside to do his daily rituals out in the fenced in back yard. I plopped myself down in a comfy chair and picked up the newspaper.

I started to read, and then re-read the same sentence... it all just blurred together. For the life of me, I couldn't concentrate. Something was gnawing at me in the back of my mind and I could not put a finger on what it was? Was it our conversation from last night or what? I just felt in my heart that I must be missing something, something.

I re-played last evening over in my mind. What was going on? Why had Gary shut down so much recently? I really felt strongly that Gary still loved me; he was just not showing me that he did, by his lack of communication. It was a terrible thought, thinking that I had let it go so far that he just became so uncommunicative. I needed to rectify this situation!

What could I do to show him that this time I was serious? We just had to get back on track with each other. I loved him so much and this distance was more than I could cope with. I needed to show him that I was not going to take this anymore; he had to understand that this time I meant business. Either he started working on our relationship or.... or what? I did not know. I didn't want to leave him, but I knew I just couldn't continue to keep this status quo. Something had to give. What??

"Rrrrrufff," Mack muffled a bark. He was patiently at the door letting me know that it was time to come in. How long was he standing outside the door watching me as I was battling with myself for an answer? *I guess I will never know*, I thought. If dogs could only talk, maybe he could help me with my dilemma?

I heard the refrigerator door open. Gary must be up, I thought. Will he come out here in the sun-room to talk to me? I waited. Of course not! Well, maybe he doesn't know where I am? *I better walk in there and see what is going on*, I thought.

"Good morning," I said as cheerfully as I could muster.

"Hi, good morning," he said and leaned over to give me a kiss. His bowl of cereal was out and he was just ready to pour the milk into it.

I kept thinking *we are both on such auto-pilot; we just are going through the usual motions. Does he really even know that I am here?*

I started getting choked up just thinking about it, but didn't want him to see that emotion right off the bat... *change the subject Jane, neutral ground please!*

"It's a beautiful day out there today, when you are done eating, would you like to go with me and take Mack for a walk around the lake?" I suggested. Behind our subdivision was a wonderful little man-made lake with a walking trail around it. "Maybe we can continue on to Starbucks too?"

"Sounds great, let me finish eating and then I will put my shoes on and we can head out. Ten minutes?" he asked.

"Fine by me and Mack will be thrilled to get a nice walk and we need to take advantage of these beautiful days," I said.

"Sure," he said.

The walk was as pleasant as I expected it to be. Mack was in his glory, having his Mom and Dad giving him such undivided attention. He was such a good guy, so laid back, but I guess most Golden Retrievers are that way. He was just such an easy dog to have and it was a pleasure walking with him. He had been so lonely since Princess had passed away the year before. Long walks would do us all a world of good.

I noticed Gary lagging behind a bit on our walk and asked, "Is everything okay?"

"Jane I am fine, just not all awake yet I guess," he quipped.

"Okay, you just seem to be walking a bit slower than usual," I stated. Something else was just a bit off, but I just couldn't pinpoint what it was. *Drop it Jane*, I thought, *you don't want to start a fight and if you keep it up, you know where it will go!*

Forty minutes later we were at Starbucks. Our usual routine was that one of us, usually me, would stake our claim to an outside table and hang out with Mack, while the other one, usually Gary, would go into Starbucks and order our coffee and snack. Just as Gary was about to enter the door to Starbucks, we heard someone calling for Gary. I turned around and scanned the parking lot and there in a distance were Diane and Bill on their bikes riding over to us.

"Why didn't you call to tell us you were going to Starbucks?" Diane asked as she got off her bike. "We rang your doorbell and your cars were both there, so we assumed that you were walking up here and we were right!"

"I'm sorry," I said. "I was just on auto-pilot this morning and never even thought of stopping by to ask, please forgive me! There are plenty of chairs today, let's grab a couple so you can join us."

Now the conversation was easy. Diane and Bill liked to talk so there was never a lull in our conversations. Bill and Gary went into Starbucks and Diane and I sat out and chatted until they returned.

"That Bill, he is just always talking about something... he never shuts up. Listen to him, bending Gary's ear! He never gives Gary a chance to talk," Diane exclaimed.

How nice that would be, I thought to myself. If I could only get Gary to say anything it would be great. I held that thought to myself.

"Want to do a cookout tonight? This weather is just fabulous and we need to take advantage of these wonderful autumn days," Diane asked.

"I don't have any plans, and I don't think Gary does, let's talk about it when the guys come back out. No wait, who am I kidding? Let's just go ahead and plan the menu, as Gary won't mind and I know we don't have any plans," I said. "I have two steaks thawing, so we could throw that on the grill."

"I have a new salad that I have been dying to make," Diane stated.

The rest of the menu was easy; we both divided up the rest.

It was just so convenient having our dear friends right next door. I loved the spontaneity of our get-togethers.

When the guys came out, laden with coffee and snacks, we 'asked' them how they felt about getting together for dinner. As we expected, they both confirmed what we thought and said yes.

"If something comes up, we will understand. Just give a call," Diane said.

"Same goes here," I stated.

"Have a nice afternoon. Bill is going to power-wash the deck. God, he is so darn obsessed with that thing! Well I guess it's better than when he power-washed the drive-way. Now that was just plain crazy!" she exclaimed. "What are you guys up to?"

"I don't know what we are doing, we haven't talked about it," I said.

"Well have fun, no matter what you do," Diane said as she put on her bike helmet. "We need to get going before this day is completely gone! See you about 5:30?"

I nodded.

They drove off and we followed behind, walking back to the house.

I had a feeling of impending doom. Why did I make plans for tonight? "Gary, was it okay that Diane and I made plans for going over to their house for dinner?"

"Sure. Why not?" he said.

We entered our front door, unleashed Mack and watched him scamper off to drink his water.

"Gary, we have to talk," I said.

"I just don't know how much more I can deal with your quietness and your lack of communication!" I stated, a bit too anxious. I just didn't know how to approach it, so I guess I just needed to blurt it out! "I just need so much more

243

in my life and you aren't willing to carry on even a simple conversation with me. Am I that uninteresting or just not to your intellect that you just don't want to talk to me?"

He stared at me, not responding. That infuriated me! Here I am trying to get him to understand and he just stares at me?

"You know, deep down I know you care, but you are just so damned quiet I can't stand it anymore!" I exclaimed, getting more emotional than I wanted to. "I just don't know what the answer is for us, where do we go from here? Every time we have this conversation, things get better for a couple of days, and then we are back in the same pattern. I feel much taken advantage of. What does it take for you to understand that this is very important to me… to us? Do you even see that there is an issue, do you even understand why I am talking to you about this?" I screamed.

"Jane, I know that this is important to you. I don't know what to do. You know I am quiet, you have always known that," he said.

"Well," I said, "quiet is one thing, but by your doing that, you are affecting our relationship and it is as if you don't care, you just expect me to deal with it. The problem is I need much more than what you are willing to give me, I guess. If you are telling me that this is just how you are and I am supposed to accept it, well you are very very wrong."

The heat was rising in my body and I could feel my face flushing bright red. I was not backing down now. The cards were on the table and he was just going to have to hear it all.

I then told him, "But you know what, as crazy as it is and why, I don't know, I do love you and I want US! I want a normal relationship where we are interested in each other and have normal conversations like normal couples. Our children are grown and out of the house and we should be enjoying time with each other and it's just not there! We are in such a rut. I feel like we are just going through the motions!"

"Do you have any idea what we can do to remedy this?" I asked.

He shook his head and said, "I don't know. I will work on being more talkative to you, I promise."

"You say that all of the time and as I said before, it gets better and then we slip right back into the same mode. I think we need to do something more drastic," I told him.

"And what would that be?" he asked.

"I think I want one of us to move out," I blurted. "Living under the same roof, just means we continue doing the same thing. We need to make a complete change so you understand that this time I really mean business.

"What?" he exclaimed. "How are we going to do that? How would being apart get us to be closer? This makes no sense!"

"What I mean is I want to date you! I don't want to be with anyone else, I just want to start getting to know you again. I just don't think it is possible to do that under the same roof. We have tried that before and it hasn't worked. There is something terribly wrong and I will be honest with you, I am miserable," I said.

"We have our motor home," I said. "One of us could move into it temporarily and then we could just begin to date each other again and get to know each other and not have the same pressures of home."

"Well, I don't see how that would work at all. I would think that dating you from here would be just the same," he said.

I stood up, tears welling in my eyes and walked out, and up to our bedroom, very upset. I closed the door and just sat on the bed thinking, *he didn't really hear me, he doesn't really get how serious this is at all! Doesn't he get it? Doesn't he want to fight for our marriage? Is this just all one sided?* I started pacing around in our bedroom. The more I paced the angrier I became. *How dare he treat this so lightly? This is our life! Damn him, why doesn't he ever show any freaking emotion!*

I heard him coming up the stairs several minutes later. He knocked quietly at the door. "Jane, please can I come in? We have to talk." I could tell that he was pretty upset; his voice was cracking as he talked.

I went over to the bed and sat down; trying to get my composure, though I knew it was really too late for that. "The door is not locked, come in," I said.

He walked in and it was very obvious that he had taken this quite seriously as tears were streaming down his cheeks. He walked over to the bed and looked down at me and said, "Jane, you can't leave me now, not now!"

I said, "What does that mean? What do you mean not now?"

He said, "You just cannot leave now, I'm really going to need your help. I think that there is something terribly wrong with me. I have had some strange symptoms for a while, a long while, and as much as I have tried to pretend that they weren't there, they are and I think I know what it is," he said, with such sadness. He then sat down at the foot of the bed and looked intently into my eyes.

"You are telling me that the reason you have been the way you are is that something is wrong with you?" I asked incredulously.

"I think it is Parkinson's disease," he blurted.

"Excuse me?" I asked. "You have had these symptoms for a while and you now decide because I pushed you into a corner to finally tell me what it is?" I was furious! *He had these symptoms for a while? He had been worrying about it*

246

for a while and he didn't tell me?

"What the heck?" he yelled. "I pour my heart out to you and all you do is say… that? I thought you would be more sympathetic to me!"

He stood up and turned and stomped out of the room, slamming the door behind him.

My mind felt like it was in overdrive. I was having a hard time focusing on the issues at hand. What the hell just took place? My mind was whirling. Parkinson's? He has had these symptoms for a while? He didn't know me at all if he thought I didn't care! I just couldn't grasp the fact that he had kept it from me! I tried to re-gain my composure and went into the bathroom and splashed some cold water on my face. *Get a grip Jane. Now isn't the time to leave, you have to go talk to him and figure out the next step.*

I walked downstairs and went to look for him. He was sitting on the sofa, with his head between his hands.

"Gary, of course I will be there for you," I said as I sat down next to him taking hold of his hand. "I just needed to process what you were saying. I still can't understand why you kept this from me for so long!"

"I just didn't want to admit it out loud to myself," he cried. "If I admit it out loud it becomes real and I just didn't want to. You know what, you noticed it last night."

"I did? What do you mean?" I asked.

"You asked me why I didn't use a spoon when I twirled my spaghetti."

"What does that have to do with Parkinson's?" I questioned.

"When you noticed that I started to think about it and realized that it has been getting more difficult to do things like that. Now YOU were even noticing, so I went on line after you went upstairs and looked up the symptoms again and sure enough, that is one of the signs," he said. "Using the fork for twirling becomes impossible. There are other symptoms too. I've noticed a slight hand tremor. I thought for a long time it was carpal tunnel syndrome. You know that, as remember I was using a brace? It didn't get any better and now the tremor is getting more noticeable."

"I do remember that," I said, "but you stopped using the brace, so I thought it was better, but I guess I just didn't notice."

"I'll admit I have been hiding the tremor," he said. "When I notice it, it is usually when I am a bit nervous or have to really use the bathroom so I put my hand in my pocket so no one sees it. I did keep that from you, and I am sorry."

He looked up at me and grabbed my hand and tears started to freely fall. I couldn't hold back my tears either and I started crying. I put my arms around him and held him and let him cry.

"Gary, I notice when you walk; your right arm doesn't swing. Is that one of the symptoms?" I asked.

"Unfortunately it is one of the symptoms. You have been noticing things also, but were just putting it out of your mind too," he said.

"I don't think we should have one of us move out," I said. "We have to figure out if this really is Parkinson's first and then go from there. Have you talked to a doctor about this?"

"No, I haven't as I have been too scared to go," he admitted.

"We will go together, if that is okay with you," I said. "We will get through this <u>together</u> Gary but I don't want you to think that I am forgetting about all I said too, we have to still continue to work on us, okay? Will you be willing to go talk to someone, like a marriage counselor?"

"I need to figure first what is going on with me. You are

right. I need to check it out and I want you to go with me.
I will really need your support," he pleaded. "As for the
counselor, I do understand that this is important to you, I
mean us, so yes. If you can find someone I am willing to do
this, but as I said, let's get in to see someone first about my
symptoms."

We would go from there. We were talking and I would
make sure we kept talking as painful as the conversations
might become. I didn't move out, but I didn't back down
either. We needed to get our relationship in order if we were
going to face this disease and the rest of our lives together.

"Gary, do you still want to go over to have dinner with Di
and Bill?" I asked.

"I do," he said, "but I don't want to tell them anything yet.
We don't know anything and there is no reason to speculate
with them. It will be good to be with them, it always is.
They will distract us and we will laugh and get our minds off
of it, even if it is for just the evening."

He looked down into my eyes, then he offered his hands
and I took them and came into a full embrace. "Thank you,
I don't know how I'd make it without you," he said softly, I
could hear the tears in his voice.

With my face pressed against his shoulder, I could hear his
heart beat, strong and steady. We'd get through this. I wasn't
sure how, but I somehow I knew we would. This was just
one more obstacle to overcome. And in my life, there had
been many, my first husband, my mother, Jared, Ben and all
the other creeps like him. This was just one more hurdle and
I would do it.

"Helloooo, Mom… MOM! Are you there?" yelled
Elizabeth, into the phone. "What is going on? You seem so
distracted!"

"Oh sorry, I was just deep in thought. Nothing to worry

about sweetheart, just a lot on my mind." *Ooh did that sound wrong? Would she figure out that something really is on my mind? Why did I have to say 'Nothing to worry about'? That made it fairly ominous!*

"What's going on? What's on your mind?"

"Nothing at all Lizzie," I tried to make my voice as slow and steady and positive as I could, but if anyone would figure it out, it would be Elizabeth. She and I always seemed to be very tuned into to each other's moods, even over the phone.

The last thing that she needed to worry about was her father's illness. Elizabeth was in third trimester of pregnancy, and we, Gary and I, decided that it was better to wait to tell her the news until after she delivered the baby. Plus, we didn't have any news yet; we still hadn't met with the neurologist.

"Just one more month and our little Madison will be meeting us! How's the last month of pregnancy going? Everything all set for the big day?" I asked, hoping my maneuvering the conversation would stop her from questioning me.

"If I made it through the summer in the North Carolina heat, I can handle about anything," she said. "It's still hot, that is for sure, but much better than it was. I just am hoping that this last month will be nice and cool as trying to carry around this baby in the heat is exhausting!"

"I hear you," I said. "I delivered both you and Ian in the summer. So I do know something about carrying a baby during the summer!"

"Mom, you know that you changed the subject, I can tell something is up," she muttered.

"Don't worry Lizzie, I'm fine. I am just trying to figure out my schedule at work so I can be with you after Madison is born and right now it is a bit of a challenge. Thank goodness we know when Maddie is coming. I guess that's one good thing about planning a cesarean!" I hated to keep something from Elizabeth, but she just didn't need that extra stress in her life right now.

"Well, you sound as if you were ready to cry," she stated. *How perceptive she is*, I thought!

"They must be tears of joy for my new granddaughter I get to spoil!" I exclaimed.

Elizabeth chuckled, "Oh Mom, you are nuts!"

We ended the conversation quite pleasantly and at least for a while my charade seemed to be holding.

Our next step was the visit to the neurologist to confirm our worries. *Maybe it wasn't Parkinson's,* I thought. Maybe it was just some sort of anomaly? He didn't deserve having one more thing as he already has bladder and prostate issues not to mention the countless surgeries to remove pre-cancerous lesions from all over his body, from being in the sun too much as a kid.

I had to stay positive. *First things first, a visit to the neurologist tomorrow*. At least we would know and we could start figuring out what to do next. We just seemed to be in a limbo pattern and I was ready to move on. Plus I had made an appointment with a counselor for the following Tuesday evening. I was determined to get our lives in order.

We drove to Walter Reed Army Medical Center the next day, Thursday, in utter silence. For some reason, the quietness was just what I needed. We were both so caught up in emotion and we needed time to process everything.

Out of the blue Gary said, "Jane, if we talk about it, it makes it real. At least for a few minutes I can bury my head in the sand and pretend that none of this exists."

I patted his arm, tears welling up in my eyes, "this might be the only time I don't mind if you are quiet. I'm feeling pretty much the same as you too… this is a tough thing Gary," I said. I glanced over and saw his face contort a bit and his eyes fill with tears. "I'm there for you, you know, every step of the way. We will get through this".

His eyes stared straight ahead at the road. I decided it was best not to say anymore as any word we had been saying lately had brought us both to tears. I let him calm down; get his body into a rhythm. I didn't want him to be all flustered when he walked into the building.

The visit with Dr. Wong, was a long and drawn out event. After waiting to see her, which seemed to be an eternity, we were more than ready to get this visit underway. She first did an intake questionnaire, discussing his symptoms and illnesses and medications. That part alone took one hour. Then she put him through all of the motions, literally. Parkinson's is a movement disorder, so she made him move, watching his gait when he walked. "Dr. Matteson, I notice that you do not swing your right arm when you walk," she commented.

"I know," Gary said. "That's been bothering me and when I concentrate on it, I can get it to swing, it's just a lot of work. The same thing goes with my right hand tremor; I can control it if I have to, or if not, I just put my hand in my pocket."

She tested his balance, his hand/eye coordination, his sense of smell. It went on and on. "I'll be back in a few minutes," Dr. Wong said, "I want to discuss this with my colleagues".

The waiting and the length of this exam were exhausting. We were feeling pretty numb. Gary was just about complete getting his clothes on, the last thing was his shoes, when Dr. Chow walked in. "Have a seat," she said.

She sat at her desk, reviewed her paperwork, and checked the computer for what seemed like an eternity. Finally she swung her chair around to face us and said, "Dr. Matteson, you are correct. I feel that you are in the early stages of Parkinson's. You still have a great amount of mobility and…"

She kept going on and on, but my mind stopped processing her comments after she told us that he had Parkinson's. I sat there numb. Oh my God, it's real. I was still questioning if it was true or not and she just blurts it out!

We returned home, feeling shell shocked. Gary's worries had now become our reality. I decided to not dwell on the negativity and the feeling sorry for ourselves and would sit at the computer for hours, learning about the disease and what we could do to improve his odds.

I found a Parkinson's clinical trial in the area at George Washington University. They were testing the drug, Rasagaline (Azilect), and it's affects on recently diagnosed individuals to see if it would slow the progression of the disease. Gary agreed to be part of this trial and was in the trial for over a year. To this day he is still taking that same medication. We are both in agreement that he most likely was on the medication (it was a blind study, so they never told us for sure if he really was on it) as it did help in slowing the progression of his disease.

I also diligently worked on finding a marriage counselor. We met with her in the evenings once a week for several months. It truly helped, but what I think helped the most was our commitment to each other to attend to these weekly sessions. Afterwards we would find a nearby restaurant to have dinner. Something was changing, something positive, we were communicating, and conversations would easily flow. I was finally getting my husband back!

Several changes began to happen in our relationship. We started going out once a week, just the two of us and called it *Date Night*. We needed time with just the two of us, away from home, away from the daily routine. In the evenings, instead of turning on the television, we decided to read to each other. It was so much fun, trying to do the voices of the different characters. We found ourselves laughing a lot. We tried everything, and it worked!

At first Gary informed me that it was a very difficult process for him, trying to open up and talk, but as time went on he admitted that it wasn't as challenging to come up with conversation. He was adapting and it was such an important and critical time in his life and mine to work on it.

We searched for a Parkinson's support group in our area and were in luck to find a great one! This has been very beneficial for Gary. He has a lot to offer the group, being a Family Physician. The group asks him many questions and I think he enjoys being able to share his medical expertise.

We are coping with this illness. I am heartbroken for him that he has to go through it, but by going through it, it has become a turning point in our lives, and has brought us much closer together. Little did I know how important this process was for us was and how much we would desperately need each other when we were faced with his next big challenge three years later.

CHAPTER 25

White Cells

*Is this part of the dark load? It has a floral pattern and
I'm not sure how to classify it*, I thought. I was obsessing
and deep in thought and barely heard that Gary had answered
the phone. *Why is there so much laundry for this time of
year? It's just the end of August and I feel I am doing an
insurmountable amount.* Our laundry seems like a never-
ending battle, though I am sure that everyone feels that at
one time or another. Thank goodness Gary does his own
laundry, but still there is always a lot to do as I do my laundry
and everything else, to include the sheets and towels. I was
feeling irritable as I frequently do when I have to do laundry.
It is such a mundane task, but one that has to be done.

I quickly became caught up in his conversation.

"Elevated?" I heard Gary say. "I know it's just routine
to check it again, yeah, you are right, it's probably just some
sort of glitch, but I will go in tomorrow for a repeat. What
did you say the level was? Really, that is quite odd. Maybe
it's my meds that I am on for Parkinson's. Yup, you are right,
we won't know until I come back in for more blood. I feel
like a pin cushion!"

I paused from the sorting and turned to Gary when he got
off of the phone and asked, "Gary, what's going on?"

"Oh nothing, I'm sure, this happens all of the time. My
white cells are elevated for some reason."

"When did you get your blood drawn and why," I asked.

"It's just my yearly stuff, I had a blood draw today," he
explained. "Since I'm on all of this medication, they want
to check my blood levels. It's a bit odd that the WBC was
elevated. It was last year too, but they did a repeat and
everything was fine."

"Well get it checked out, we don't need one more thing right now and I just want to make sure that all is okay, okay? Can you get it done tomorrow?" I tried to casually mention this, trying not to sound alarmed.

"Yeah, I can. Thank goodness I can get it done at the clinic at the Pentagon so I won't have to go too far out of the way."

I went back to my sorting, mulling over the phone conversation. I wasn't going to obsess about it, as really, it was probably nothing. Then I pondered, *if I hadn't heard the phone call, would he have told me?* I knew that we, Gary and I, were doing much better with our communication than we had three years earlier prior to Gary's Parkinson's diagnosis. In the three years, conversation had definitely improved, though it still had a long way to go.

"I know you think this is nothing, Gary, but please let me know when you get the results, okay?" I asked. "I really don't want to slip back into old habits."

"Jane, I promise. I learned my lesson three years ago!" he said defiantly.

"What was your white blood cell count this time?" I asked.

He looked at me, and then quickly looked away. *I know that look, that is his worried look*, I thought.

"Around 22,000," he said. "But don't worry, it's the meds I am almost sure of it. That's why they monitor my blood levels because of all that crap I am on for Parkinson's and my bladder."

Okay, he is a doctor and he knows these things, right? Jane, stop worrying! I thought. *Just let it go or you will make him nervous too.*

259

What the heck is the normal level I wondered? I know
I am a nurse, but that isn't part of what I do daily at work
and though I know I had to learn the different levels a long
time ago, I just didn't remember them now. I would have to
Google it and see.

I painstakingly took my time with the laundry. I didn't
want to rush to the computer so Gary would see that I was
worried. Within a half an hour I completed as much as I
could and I leisurely strolled over to the computer to check
my email. I couldn't make it obvious that I was researching.
I typed in the Google search bar, *WBC normal levels*.
Within seconds, there were over a million results.
Click, pause... wait.

I audibly gasped!

"What's wrong?" Gary asked.

Well, so much for my keeping it to myself, I thought.
"Gary, WBC normal levels are from 3.8-10.8. Twenty-two
thousand, wow that is really elevated!"

"I know, but please don't worry," he said. "Things like
this happen all the time and it doesn't mean anything, really.
We just have to wait and see and then go from there."

"Easy for you to say," I quipped.

We had a lovely dinner, salmon on the grill, Caprese salad
and chilled white Pinot Grigio. I geared our conversation
towards a lighthearted one thinking in the back of my mind
that it was the best thing to do, not bringing up the blood
work again. I would re-address it tomorrow after he got
home from work and after the blood draw.

I refused to let the phone call from the doctor bother me
and kept myself busy. The following day was Friday, which
just happened to be my day off. *Let's see how can I keep
myself busy*, I thought? *Lunch with my friend Treena, now
that would be perfect*! Thankfully Treena was available and I

knew she would be a great distracter!

We met at our usual restaurant, the Cedar Café and had our Chicken Shawarma Sandwiches and sat there for over two hours discussing life. There was never a lack of conversation when talking to Treena. We have known each other since about 1994. Her husband, Jeff, was also a retired military Colonel and we all just kept getting assigned to the same military posts several times in our spouse's military careers. It was great just sitting there with her and letting the conversations flow in any direction they wanted to. I was so lucky to have her in my life.

Treena knew me though and sensed right away that something was up. "Jane, what is up? You seem pretty distracted. Is Gary's Parkinson's getting worse?"

Of course she would notice, she has seen me through the good and the bad, I couldn't keep anything from her. "Oh, we are just waiting on some blood results. Gary said not to worry, but I am, of course! I mean really, how could I not worry?" I exclaimed.

"I'm glad he is talking to you about it Jane as I know there were times, not all that long ago, that he would have kept that from you," she stated.

"I know. He's being a lot better about it. Let's change the subject so I quit worrying, okay?" I requested. "Anything… how are your boys doing?"

"Oh you know my boys, there are *always* stories," she grinned. "How long did you say you have to today, as this could take a long time?"

I sat back and listened. *Ahh, just what I needed,* I thought. That was the great thing about Treena, we both listened to each other, it wasn't just a one sided relationship. I smiled.

My frame of mind lightened significantly after talking to Treena. The rest of the day just flew by as I ran errands, gassed and washed the car and even made it to the Fort Belvoir Commissary to do my grocery shopping. It was a productive Friday!

I never know when Gary will arrive home from work, some days it is 6:30, but most days it is 7:00 or way after. It's always hard to plan a meal, but I do the best I can. *Hmmm, what could I make that we wouldn't have to worry about too much,* I thought. *I know, he always loves my spaghetti! That will be easy and with a quick salad, it would make it perfect!*

The phone rang and I picked it up, "Hello," I said.

"Is Colonel Matteson in please, this is Dr. Brown."

"Hi Dr. Brown, no but I expect him any minute to arrive home from work. Can I take a message?" I nervously asked.

"Well tell him I would like to talk to him tonight. I will be at the office for another hour or so. He has my number," he said.

"I can do that," I said. "I expect he will give you a call in a few minutes".

Oh, I did not like Dr. Brown's tone of voice, not at all! *Okay Jane, remain calm,* I thought. *We don't know anything yet.*

I put myself to work and was busy chopping onions and peppers when Gary arrived home. I knew that Gary must have just opened the garage door by the way our two dogs were reacting. They always let us know when anyone comes within 500 feet of the house! It was a cacophony of sound! Fergus, the Border Collie, was barking repeatedly and Womack, the Golden Retriever was howling. I just wanted to scream at them to stop, but I knew that it was only my nerves reacting. They would calm down when they saw their Daddy.

The door to the kitchen from the garage opened. "Hi," Gary said. "I'm finally home, sorry it took so long, I had to stop and get gas."

I didn't want to immediately discuss the phone call with Gary, but time was of the essence, he needed to call Dr. Brown before he left work for the day. "Gary, Dr. Brown called about 10 minutes ago and wants you to call him back as soon as you can. Crap, Gary, I don't like this at all. I didn't like his attitude when he called," I said.

"Jane, we don't know anything, STOP worrying, please. This doesn't help anyone!" he pleaded.

"Okay, you are right, sorry," I stammered. "But please call now before he leaves please."

Gary reached for his cell phone to get Dr. Brown's number and then dialed the number. "Hi Dr. Brown, it's Gary Matteson, Jane tells me you called. Did you get my results of the blood work I did today? Really? Still not down? Hmm, that is unusual. Still I think it has something to do with my meds I am on. Referral? Okay, I can do that. I guess you are right, that is the next step. Okay you put the referral in and I will get the appointment set up. Thanks so much for taking care of this." He slowly placed his phone down on the counter.

"Okay, here is the deal, the WBC's are still elevated, 21,500, so he wants to put a referral in for me to be seen at Walter Reed," he stated.

"Referral, to whom?" I asked.

"Hematology/Oncology, but don't stress about it, look at it as Hematology. Something is weird with my blood and they need to figure it out. I am still betting on the fact that it is something to do with my meds I am on."

"Would you like me to go with you to the appointment?" I asked.

263

"Sure," he said. "Dr. Brown is going to put the referral in, so I have to wait a few days for that to process. I will call next Wednesday and see when I can get seen. Is there anything I can help with dinner? I'm starving!"

I knew what he was doing. He was trying to act like it was nothing so I wouldn't worry. *Fat chance I wouldn't worry!* When Gary was nervous, he would eat like a horse, me on the other hand would just shut down and hardly be able to eat a bite. The food didn't look too appetizing to me now.

"No, I have it under control," I said. "Go change out of your work clothes, dinner should be about ready by the time you come down."

Of course the only word I heard was Oncology, even though Gary told me not to. *A blood problem and he needs to go to Oncology. Is it Leukemia, Lymphoma?* I thought. *My Dad had Lymphoma almost 20 years ago. No one in his family had cancer, well wait a minute, Gary's Dad had Prostate Cancer.* My mind was flooded with thoughts.

Now we wait…

How long until the diagnosis?

It seemed as if every time the phone rang recently it was bad news and here it was ringing again. I dreaded picking it up. It was too early for Gary to be home from work but I answered it in case he was calling to tell me he'd be late.

"Hello," I said into the phone.

"Hi, is Colonel Matteson there please?" asked a woman with a very pleasant feminine voice.

"No, he isn't. He is still at work, can I take a message?" I informed her.

"Is this his wife, Jane? This is Dr. Benson at Walter Reed Oncology, we've met." She said before I could respond. "I think we will postpone the bone marrow test for a while, he needs to come in to the clinic tomorrow for more blood work, especially since his last blood work is very suspicious for CLL."

"Do you have Gary's work phone number? You really need to be talking to him about this," I sounded calm but in my mind I was frantic. After I hung up, I just screamed and wailed... *NO IT CAN'T BE*! CLL?? Chronic Lymphocytic Leukemia?? It can't be!

Hasn't this doctor ever heard of HIPAA? According to HIPAA policy, she should never have told me this presumptive diagnosis over the phone, *where in the hell is patient confidentiality?* But she did tell me, and what was done was done, and I needed to move on from there.

I waited about 10 minutes, then I phoned Gary and as calmly as I could, asked if his doctor had called. He said, "I was going to tell you about the phone call when I saw you tonight, she said I should come in Friday, tomorrow, for more blood work. She said she would have a copy of my blood work, from Tuesday, waiting for me. Then she said she wants to talk to me afterwards. That also means you too, if you can come."

"Oh Gary, of course I will come. I just wish you didn't have to go through all of this! How the hell could she call and tell me that over the phone?" I blurted out realizing he didn't know she had called me first. "This is horrendous news," I wailed. "You know whatever it is I am with you every step of the way!" I added.

He remained pretty calm about it all on that Thursday night after work, stating once again that it was probably from his medications that he had been taking for his Parkinson's that was causing such a fluctuation. I felt a coil of anger, how much longer I would hear this same excuse? I knew that he was trying not to worry me. But did he really think I wasn't worried? That I couldn't see through his flimsy excuse?

I tried to temper my indignation with the understanding that he probably needed to find some plausible explanation that made some sense to him. Something he could hold onto. I knew he was worried too which probably explained why he was trying to talk himself out of it being something dire.

But in my heart, I wondered how many more blood tests did this man need before they got a diagnosis? How much more convincing did he need before he would believe something was wrong? I was beginning to lose track of how many times he had gotten his blood drawn. From my own background as an RN, I also knew it wasn't just his white blood cells, but much more detailed information was what the doctors were seeking.

Friday morning we were at Dr. Benson's to have yet another round of blood work drawn. We had barely walked into her office and sat down before she handed Gary the blood work from his last visit. From the look on her face, I saw concern. But it was Gary's reaction that really scared me. I watched as he read through the report and quickly his face turned ashen. My stomach did a flip. I really did not want to see that horrible look on his face, it meant, there was more to come… more disheartening news.

"Colonel Matteson", she said. "We know that it is some form of blood cancer and we are leaning towards CLL, though it could be a Lymphoma. We won't know for sure until you have the bone marrow biopsy done. We will also do a CT scan and both will help in staging your cancer. Can we get you scheduled for it next week?"

I know that doctors do these diagnoses for a living and

maybe that is their coping mechanism, being so nonchalant, but I just wanted to shake her. Where was the goddamn compassion? This was my husband hearing the worst news of his life! How could she be so cold?

I was so incensed that I couldn't think straight. I wanted somehow to shield him from this awful truth, to be able to look him in the eyes and say: "Everything's going to be all right," but I couldn't, because I didn't know if everything was going to be all right. I didn't even know if he was going to be with me another year as the diagnosis for CLL was extremely grim.

We left the hospital, both of us feeling despondent. Finally he owned up to his fear. He told me that after reading the lab, he had been pretty sure that he had CLL or something similar. Now he was quiet, withdrawn and emotional, all rolled into one.

I had been so concerned that he wasn't facing reality but now that he was, I had no idea how to comfort him. I was also dealing with my own emotions around this and found that I was feeling pretty despondent too. But I was chastising myself as I really felt like I had to be strong for him. I had to be our strength. My only worry was how to pull it all off and come across strong when I was feeling as if my world just crashed into a million pieces?

I did not want to just sit around and wait for this diagnosis. We needed to do *something.* Now! It served no purpose to dwell on the situation every minute. Besides, how would that change anything? It certainly wasn't helping. We had to find a way to cope.

So I encouraged him to do something fun, hoping it would give his mind a break from it all. We decided to go to the movies after the appointment. We picked *Julie and Julia.* It was a great movie, lighthearted and funny, just what we needed. I had a lump in my throat the entire time the movie was playing and cried softly to myself through a good portion of it. I made sure he did not see me but I needed a release, anyone would after being dealt such horrific news. He was unusually quiet throughout so I don't know how much of the movie he saw either, but at least we were doing something. And that had been the point. It wasn't meant to be a fix and couldn't have been one anyway.

"We will make the best we can of this situation this weekend. One day at a time is all we can do," I said. "I'm here for you." He smiled at me, but it was a sad smile that didn't reach his eyes. I knew there was a lot going on inside him but as with before, Gary was still very guarded with his feelings.

We had needed some lighthearted activities that weekend, and that we had. Diane and Bill's house was filled with so much noise and laughter on Friday, that we didn't have any time to sit and feel sorry for ourselves. We were absolutely caught up in the frivolities of food, wine, champagne, laughter and great conversations. *Just what the doctor ordered*, I thought. *Well, maybe what she should have ordered!*

The following Tuesday it was back to business. As I tidied up I heard Gary calling for me. "Jane… Jane!" He called to me.

"Oh, sorry, I was just thinking about the nice break we had this weekend with Di and Bill and everyone! Sorry I just drifted off there!" I exclaimed as I stood up suspending my vacuuming.

"No, it is a good memory and you deserve not to have to think about this cancer every minute. It is always a fun time when we all are together and God knows we need to hold on to those memories!" he stated. "By the way, the doc is going to set up my bone marrow biopsy for this Friday morning. They still didn't know if it is Lymphoma or Leukemia. Great choices, huh? If I had my way I don't think I would be picking either of those!" he said.

"I know," I told him.

"They are also going to do more blood work and a CT scan on Friday. I will have to do a 24 hour urine and give it to them when we go for the appointment on Friday. As if that's not enough, they are now working on setting up my Endoscopy and Colonoscopy for next week too. I have a feeling that you will need to take some time off work next week as I can't drive home after the colonoscopy. I hope to have that scheduled tomorrow so you can let your boss know when you need to take off time."

"No problem, my bosses are very understanding as you know. I am pretty lucky! They told me that just to let them know what time I needed off and they would make it happen," I said, standing up and walking to the kitchen. "Guess it's time to think about dinner. What sounds good to you?"

"How about no cancer?" he sarcastically laughed. "Let the tests begin!" he abruptly changed his tone as he made a fake drum roll on the coffee table.

I looked at him. He was trying so hard to be brave. I wondered if it was more for me or him. I just dreaded that he had to go through all of this. It was just so unfair. But I reminded myself: *One step at a time Jane that is all you can do.*

"Woohoo," I joked, trying to match his spirit. "Let the good times roll!" He gave me a high five but I saw it in his eyes. He was afraid, how could I blame him?... I was too.

Biopsy

I am not sure why I was dreading the bone marrow biopsy so much, but I was. Maybe it was because it was such an invasive procedure or maybe because once it was done we would soon know the answers, Gary would have the final diagnosis. In some respects, *great… bring it on and then we can work on fighting this f***ing disease!!* In other respects, I didn't want to know! I wanted to go back to how everything was before. Parkinson's disease isn't the greatest thing to have, but a blood cancer, that is a whole other story.

The CT scan was done first and then of course more blood work was done. As soon as we arrived up at Hematology/ Oncology, Gary was whisked away for the biopsy. As he was walking down the hall to the procedure, I stared at them and asked, "Gary, do you want me with you?"

"Please?" he pleaded.

"Many spouses stay for the procedure, we can put a chair up by your husband's head so you can talk with him. If you feel comfortable staying, I think it would be a great help to him to have you there," said Dr. Benson.

In walked a new doctor on the team that we hadn't met with before. It was obvious that he was quite familiar with Gary's case and he said, "Dr. Matteson, my name is Dr. Hahn, I just want to keep you up to date on what we are pretty sure you have. We are now leaning towards Mantle Cell Lymphoma. There is a genetic marker that we found in your blood, Cyclin D1, and this marker is pretty specific to Mantle Cell Lymphoma. We will explain more what this type of rare B cell Lymphoma is, but let's get the biopsy done first. The biopsy will help us get that definitive diagnosis and will help in the staging of your cancer."

Oh crap, what a thing to hear just before having that procedure done! How could I sit there, and be supportive for

Gary when I just wanted to scream? *Okay Jane, you have to be there for Gary, get a grip! Mantle Cell Lymphoma? Now what? This is not the time for me to feel sorry for myself, be there for Gary, and show him you are there for him. He must be freaked out about now!*

I grabbed the chair and moved up towards Gary's head. He was on his stomach, with his pants pulled half way down his legs. The sample is done on the iliac crest on his hip. As a nurse I was quite interested in the procedure they were about to do, as a wife I was repulsed by it and just wanted to protect Gary from such a thing! "Hey Gary, it's too bad you don't get to see this. This is cool! Nice butt!! Want me to take some pictures?" I joked.

"Oh real cool, thanks Jane. And don't think I don't know what you are doing; you are trying to relax me! Thanks, I really do need you to do that. You know I have done this biopsy before to some of my patients, but it is so different when it is you having it done! Can you just keep on talking to me please? I hate this and I hate that I have to put you through this you know," he said with a crack in his voice.

"Hey buddy, I am there for you through thick and thin. Remember our vows… for better or for worse, in sickness and in health! Don't think you are getting rid of me any time soon!" I teased.

Gary was numbed up beautifully so the procedure was not bad at all, that was until they began aspirating the bone marrow. The marrow was semi liquid so the needle used was quite large. "Damn, it feels like an electric shock just went through me!" he yelled. As quickly as the pain appeared, it was gone and he felt fine.

"A lot of tests will be done on the marrow, to include flow cytometry and chromosome analysis," said Dr. Hahn. "Have you had any lymph node involvement, sir?"

271

"No, not a bit, the only way we knew something was up was my white blood cell count was so elevated," Gary mentioned. "When will we get some results back on this?"

"Well, we still need your endoscopy and colonoscopy done, as this will tell if it has gone to your lymph system. When are you having those done?" Doctor Benson asked.

"Monday," Gary said.

"Great, the sooner the better," she said. "I would hope mid to late next week we will have all the answers. Did you already complete your 24-hour urine?"

"Yup, I turned that in bright and early this morning. So now we wait?" Gary asked.

"Yes, that is pretty much all we can do right now. Let's set up an appointment to see me next Thursday at 9:00, okay?" she asked.

"We will be there," said Gary, as he looked at me hoping I was in agreement and would be there with him. I nodded my head, and grabbed Gary's hand and gave it two quick squeezes. He squeezed back twice. (This has always been our 'I love you' sign to each other when we couldn't say it out loud.)

They applied the pressure dressing to the site and explained to Gary to keep the dressing on the rest of the day and take it off in the morning. Gary is pretty good about following doctor's orders so I wasn't too concerned.

"Still not a complete diagnosis… again," Gary said to me as we were walking out the main door of Walter Reed. We finally got to our car and Gary turned to me and said, "God damn… shit…FUCK… this absolutely sucks!!! I have a fucking rare lymphoma! How the hell did this happen to me? Why? Isn't this damn Parkinson's enough?" The tears were pouring down our faces. I stopped walking and took him in my arms and there we both stood, together, in the parking lot… sobbing. People walked by and stared, but they were pretty oblivious to us. We needed each other and this was the only thing that seemed to help at the moment.

"Okay, I have to go back to work," Gary said as he let go of our embrace.

I looked up incredulously at him. "What? You really are going back to work now? Really?"

"Jane, I can't stay home! I have to work," he said grabbing my hands. "Once we get the full diagnosis I know that there will be many days that I probably won't be able to work, you know, with the chemo and all. So please understand. I HAVE to go in. It will be better for me to go in and stay busy. It will keep my mind occupied and distracted."

I couldn't argue with that, he was right.

He looked down at me and reminded me, "Don't forget you are going on that trip with your book club today for the weekend, to Smith Mountain Lake and you have to leave soon."

"Oh crap, I forgot! I don't want to go! I don't want to leave you this weekend! How can I go, we need each other!" I pleaded.

"You do need to go Jane, these are your friends and your friends will be a huge support to you. Please promise me that you will go. There might not be any more trips you will be able to go on, once the chemo starts, so take advantage of this time. They will understand, you need to be with them."

"No, what I need is to be with you, but you are right. I will be back early Sunday morning, so it will just be two nights and really just all day tomorrow. Are you sure about this?" I asked. "I know everyone would understand if I didn't go."

"I know you are worried about me, I am too. But I will be fine… I promise and don't worry, I won't do anything stupid," he said.

"Promise?" I asked.

I could see his eyes tearing up again and he said, "I wouldn't do that to you and I am making you that promise."

It was on my mind, suicide. He immediately knew what I was concerned about. In 1992, his father had committed suicide just two days before we were to return home from our tour in Germany. His Dad had prostate cancer and it had been causing him unbearable pain, he couldn't take it anymore.

"That isn't going to happen, Jane… that is all I can say and you HAVE to believe me."

I knew deep down he was telling me the truth, but I knew he was struggling with this diagnosis and he had no one to talk to about it as we hadn't shared it with anyone yet. "I'm holding you to that. I love you so much and I want to have many more years with you!" I exclaimed.

"Really, I have to get to work now. I will be FINE! Go play for the weekend and call me a lot, okay? I will want to hear that sweet happy voice of yours! Now get in that car and go, before I change my mind!" he joked.

"Deal," I said. "I don't know how much company I will be with my friends, but I will try! Don't work too hard and remember, call me whenever you want."

"I love you," he said as he rubbed my chin with his finger. "See you Sunday morning."

"Hey you," I said as I grabbed his hand.

I gave it two squeezes, smiled and walked to my car.

Mistake

I fumbled with my cell phone lying on the front side passenger seat of my Toyota Prius. *Damn, no signal strength.* Of course there wouldn't be, I was out on back country roads. An hour ago I had snuck out the front door of Fay's beautiful vacation home at Smith Mountain Lake just as the clock was chiming 7:00 a.m., leaving the book club women sleeping soundly in their beds. Was it too early to give Gary a call? I wanted him to know that I was on my way. It was a long drive, over four and a half hours and I knew that I needed an early start. As wonderful a time as I had with my friends, I knew where I needed to be, home with Gary.

It was a beautiful drive home from the lake, but the back roads were slow. Any other day I would have enjoyed the beauty that was all around me on that crisp morning but today I was looking for an interstate to get me home quicker. Unfortunately the interstate was nowhere near where I was headed. Route 29 was the quickest way. *Come on truck, what are you doing on the road so early? Crap, 35 in a 55? Give me a break here, please??*

Relax Jane, he is okay! You just talked to him last night before bed. He had tried to sound upbeat when we talked, but I could still sense his sadness. "What have you guys been up to today, fun no doubt, right?" he asked.

"We had a very full day," I told him. Five of the nine women that are in the book club made it to the Lake. "We went to a wine festival for a couple of hours, but it was raining too hard and we were getting drenched so we came home and watched a movie. Oh yeah, and then last night Fay told us about a fabulous restaurant that she just loved, so we went and it was delicious! Oh, and did I mention our pillow fight?" What a great distracter they had been for me.

"No, I can't say I remember that and I think I would have," Gary teased.

"We were being pretty silly and had a fake pillow fight. I took tons of pictures. Isn't that what you do at a sleep-over, have a pillow fight?" I joked.

"My guess is that alcohol was involved?" Gary asked.

"Why would you ever say that?" I joked. "Well, maybe just a tad!" I knew what Gary was doing, and I knew he was most likely miserable at home by himself, but he was putting up a façade as he didn't want to ruin my time. I just needed to get home and see for myself how he was doing.

Finally, at 11:30 in the morning I rounded the corner into our neighborhood. I was nervous, I didn't know what to expect. My stomach lurched as I swung into the drive way. *What was I going to find? Remember, you just talked to him last night and he was fine.* I kept telling myself. I felt the butterflies in my stomach.

I grabbed my overnight bag and went through the back door. "Gary?" I called out. Nothing. "Gary," I said a bit louder. Nothing. *Okay, take a deep breath Jane, he is probably just upstairs in the bathroom and he can't hear you!*

"Hey there, Mack and Fergus!" I said to my two dogs that were waiting for me when I opened the back door. "Where's your Daddy, is he upstairs?" I asked, knowing they would just keep on wagging their happy tails, oblivious to my questions.

I bounded up the stairs two at a time and reached our bedroom in about two seconds flat. "Gary?" I said at the door.

"I'm here," he said in a very weak voice. There he was, standing in the middle of the room, hair disheveled, with a two day beard growth. He took one look at me and burst into tears.

Oh God, I thought, *what is going on?*

"Gary, look at me, please. Did something happen? Gary, look at me!" I grabbed his face between my hands and lifted his head so I could look into his eyes.

Tears were streaming down his face. "I don't know what to do, I just don't know! I am miserable. Why in the hell has this happened? Not only do I have Parkinson's but now I have been given cancer! I'm a fucking train wreck!!"

"You are NOT a train wreck, you hear me!" I said still staring intently into his eyes. "Oh God, I knew I never should have gone on this trip, I should never have gone, you needed me and I wasn't there!" I cried.

We stood there in the middle of the bedroom holding each other and crying, with both dogs at our heels trying to demand their own attention. "I love you," I whispered in his ear "and we are going to get through this together, you got that? We can fight anything as long as we are together and we always will be together. I am so sorry I left you this weekend, especially when you were the most vulnerable. Can you ever forgive me for leaving you? You needed me and I wasn't there for you and I'm just sick about it."

"I didn't realize how much I really did need you this weekend, Jane. It has felt like the weekend from hell for me," he said sobbing, "though much of it I feel like I was in a fog. But I didn't want to be selfish and I truly DID want you to be able to get away and enjoy yourself. God, I need your touch and your hugs. I really, really need it. This is beginning to make me feel better already."

"I'm so sorry I wasn't here for you," I cried. "You do know that this is where I wanted to be?"

"I know," he said while wiping a tear streaming down my face, "I guess I just didn't think I was going to have such a tough time of it."

"We haven't told anyone so you had to deal with all of this yourself all weekend. I wish our kids knew that something was going on, as they could have been here for you, especially Ian and Jenny since they live so close. It had to be overwhelming for you," I said.

"You know me, I wouldn't have talked to anyone anyhow, plus they are busy planning Sam's baptism and they don't need to deal with this," he sniffed, trying to catch his breath, "they don't want to hear my sad stories".

"I don't think that is true, but I know we decided to wait until you had the full diagnosis," I said, "so this had to be extra hard. I'll tell you what, let me fix you something to eat while you get in the shower and clean up. Have you showered this weekend, shaved or brushed your teeth?" I tried to calmly ask. I didn't want him to sense how appalled I was with his disheveled appearance.

"I guess I never thought to do that," he grinned slightly. "Now I have a reason to, you are home."

Family Support-Decisions

"Hey Ian," I said into the phone. "How are you guys doing?"

"Whazzup Momma J??" Ian joked.

"Oh, I have just been thinking about you guys and I know what a busy time this is right now for you guys, with the approaching baptism of Sam this weekend. I'm here to offer my support in any way I can!"

"Thanks Mom. Jenny really has got it under control, she is amazing like that, you know? Now, what you could help with, if only anyone could, is to help us figure out a way that Sammie would sleep through the night! If you could do that, we would be forever in your debt! Poor Jenny gets up several times a night. I know... I know what you are thinking Mom, why aren't I getting up too?"

I chuckled, "Well, the thought did cross my mind!"

"I do get up frequently on the weekends and also let Jenny sleep in on those days I'm off. We have a schedule for that and I promise I am not a slacker!" he said.

"Well good," I exclaimed. "I'm glad to hear that my son is being a good father and husband. Kudos to you! Slackers are not allowed!"

"No worries, I promise. Hey what's up with you, you sound a bit low, am I right?" Ian asked.

Ahh my perceptive son, I thought. *No Jane, this is not the time to discuss the diagnosis with him. They have a houseful of guests coming in two days and the last thing they need to do right now is worry about Gary.*

My mind was drifting back to last week's meeting at the hospital. "Jane, I think I am in stage three," Gary said, while waiting for Dr. Benson to come in to the exam room.

"What makes you say that?" I asked. "Why don't we just wait until Dr. Benson comes in and lets us know? Do you think all of the results are in?"

"I do, because she would have changed the appointment if all the results weren't yet available. That's how she operates."

The door opened and in walked a smiling Dr. Benson. *Oh, I thought, is there any glimmer of hope here?* I knew I was grasping at straws. Maybe the bone marrow was fine and his blood was mixed up with someone else and she was going to say. We were wrong, you are fine! And then.... the dreaded words.

"Well, we have the majority of the test results back sir,"

she said. "Your blood work continues to show Mantle Cell, as you know with that genetic marker, Cyclin D1. All of the reports are in. Your colonoscopy is clear, odd though as usually something shows up in the colon. Your spleen is slightly enlarged."

"What about the bone marrow?" Gary urged.

She glanced at her paperwork in front of her and started reading numbers aloud that literally had no meaning to us. Then I thought I heard the words, but it was as if she was giving a weather report *cloudy with a chance of Mantle Cell*? No, what was she saying? "Because of the presence in the bone marrow you are considered stage four. Oh, the 24 hour urine is normal. We need to set up an appointment with your team to figure out the next step."

Did she really just say in a matter of fact tone, oh *by the way, you are in stage 4?*

"So Mom, what is up with you, you are just a bit distracted," Ian said.

"Oh, just stuff going on here. Dad and I have something to talk to you and Jenny about and thought next week after this baptism is finished we could go out to dinner," I said.

"Mom, you are scaring me here, what the heck is going on?"

"Nothing that can't wait, really, so what day next week works for you? Monday or Tuesday?" I asked.

"Let me check with Jenny and I'll give you a call back. I love you Mom."

"You are loved too. Give my grandson a hug for me!" I said.

Five minutes later the phone rang. "Mom, we don't want to wait until after the baptism. If there is something you need to discuss, let's meet sooner. How about this evening?" Ian asked. "Jenny and I thought that maybe you could come over a bit earlier and spend some 'Umma" time with Sam before Dad gets here. Maybe he can just come over on his way home from work?"

Crap, that isn't what they need to hear right now I thought, as I ended the conversation. I told him I would call his dad and see what plans we could make.

We, Gary and I, decided that meeting at a restaurant was probably not a good plan. We met them over at their home about four hours after the phone call. The plan was to order pizza, but no one ever thought about food after our conversation.

I was sitting on the floor with Sam and watching him play with his toys when Gary just blurted out, "I have something to tell you and the only way to do it is just get it out quickly, I have cancer, stage 4 Lymphoma, Mantle Cell Lymphoma."

The silence in the room could have been cut with a knife.

One of the more difficult things for me is to see Gary cry, and when the tears started streaming down his face, I thought I was going to lose it right there. I reached for his hand and just held it. Ian came up behind Gary and put his arm around him and then Jenny grabbed his other hand. There we were, a big cocoon of protection and love. We were silent for the next few moments, each caught up in our own thoughts.

"God, Dad I didn't even know anything was going on!" Ian exclaimed.

"We knew you had so much going on, with Sam's baptism. We didn't want to worry you," Gary said. "We really did want to wait until after the baptism."

"Dad," Ian said, "get real, we have to know this stuff. You *have* to keep us informed! No one should keep something like this to themselves. How long has it been that you have known something was wrong?"

"Really, we just found out, and he has been going through the tests for about a month now," I told them. "You know, he had no idea anything was going on until he had routine blood work drawn and his white blood cell count was elevated. He's been having a plethora of tests trying to determine what it is."

"What the heck is this lymphoma?" Ian said. "I haven't heard of this."

"You are not alone," I said, "we hadn't either. Even though we are both in the medical profession, oncology or cancer is definitely not our field of expertise. This is new to us too."

Jenny was very quiet, playing with Sammie, handing him a stuffed teddy bear. I understood what she was doing; she was trying to busy herself to keep things together. I sensed she was really struggling with this news as she loved Gary as much as Ian did.

Ian was trying to be so strong, ask all of the right questions, but I could tell in his voice that this news was just tearing him apart. He ran his fingers through his hair and asked, "So now you know, what is next? When does treatment start?"

"We really don't know the next step yet," Gary said. "We have to meet with the group that is assigned to my case next week and hear what they have to say. They have a few options for us. Watchful waiting, chemo and chemo with autologous stem cell transplant."

"Well, I hope this will start soon, I don't want you to wait another second!" Ian exclaimed. "What in the world is autologous?"

I piped in, as I knew this was tough for Gary. "It is stem cells from one's own blood and bone marrow. I had to research this as well, as I had no idea what it meant.

Really once we know what is going on we will tell you, we promise. I imagine that within the next month things will be happening."

"I hope you aren't thinking of watchful waiting?" said Ian.

"It's not the plan, but I," Gary said while looking directly into my eyes, "er …we, need to get the full picture from the doctors before we decide what is best."

"Mom, Dad thanks for telling us as I know that you wanted to wait a bit," Ian said. "God, I just can't imagine what you are going through, both of you! Promise you will keep us informed every step of the way. This is just so freaking unfair. I love you guys so much you know?"

"I love you too!" Jenny piped in and gave us a hug.

We all decided to pass on having dinner together as we could tell that Ian and Jenny just needed time with each other to process what they were just told. I knew that many tears would be shed after we left their house. Ian was being so brave, but I saw it in his face that he was struggling to keep it together. There he was, holding Sam in his one arm and the other wrapped around Jenny. *Who was holding who up?*

I grabbed Gary's hand as we walked out their front door and said, "Now it's time for you to tell Elizabeth."

Elizabeth and I had been talking and she knew what was going on. I needed someone to talk to during all of this chaos and she was there for me, every step of the way. It was great to have her to vent my concerns and worries. We had to keep the Parkinson's from her until after her delivery of Maddie; I just couldn't keep this from her now. What she didn't know was the complete diagnosis and also she hadn't talked to her father about it at all. I hated that it had to be a phone conversation, but she was living in North Carolina and we just couldn't take a trip down there right now. Too much was happening for Gary here.

"I know Jane, and I do want to talk to her, but I hate like hell to upset her with this. God, I hate like hell to have to tell anyone!" Gary said, while leaning against his car. "Why can't we just one time have some good news? Why the hell does it have to be this way?"

"Do you want to tell her before the baptism, since she will be here in two days?" I asked.

"I do, I really do. I am not going to keep this one to myself, like I did with the Parkinson's, I know that I need all of the support I can get right now. I will give her a call tonight," he said.

"Gary, just to let you know, she has some knowledge of what is going on, I had to have someone to talk to and she has been so supportive," I told him. "She just doesn't have the whole story yet."

He looked deep into my eyes and said, "I didn't know that the two of you had been talking."

"I'm sorry, she is the only one that knows and please, you have to understand, I needed someone that would listen," I explained. "She is so worried and I really did hate to burden her with this but I have also been going through hell worrying about you! I know that we were keeping this close hold, don't be upset with me!"

He put his arms around my waist and pulled me to him and said, "I can't be upset with you, and I really do totally understand. It's just not me going through this, you have so much to deal with too, and I have been selfish." I watched his eyes as a tear slowly slid down his face. "You shouldn't have to put up with all of this!"

"Gary, there is nowhere else I would want to be and you know that. Thanks for understanding about Elizabeth, but you aren't off the hook, she still needs to talk to you, okay?"

"I promise to give her a call tonight, I said I would and I will and even though she partially knows, this will still be a hard phone call to make," he said. "I know I have a lot of calls to make and we need to start letting family and friends know. I don't know about you, but I am starved! We never had our dinner with Ian and Jenny, I understand why, but man I need to get some food!"

I laughed, "That's so you, Gary, in a crisis you eat. Me, well I just shut down and have no desire for food, but if you're hungry I'm all for it. I just want to be with you, so let's go, any ideas where you want to eat?"

Choices

I precariously balanced two cups of tea in my hands as I slowly walked into the living room. I put a cup out for Gary to take and noticed my hand was trembling with worry. I watched as Gary held his head in his hands and shook it back and forth.

"God, Jane, what awful decisions we have to make! Both of our choices sound like hell, but we have to decide the best plan of attack for this cancer." We had just left the Cancer Institute at NIH (National Institutes of Health) and had talked to another fantastic team of doctors.

He glanced up at me and saw the tea and grabbed it from me and gave me a grimace. "Thanks for the tea, though something stronger would be good too!"

"Later, we have a lot to talk out and I don't want our minds fogged up with alcohol. Let's sit down and rationally try to decide what the best decision is for you. You do know that this is ultimately YOUR decision right? I can help you with this as much as you want," I said while slowly sipping my tea, "but the final decision has to be yours."

He patted the seat next to him for me to sit down and said, "We are deciding this together. You are always telling me that we are a team, remember? I do know and understand what you are saying though and I appreciate it."

I sat down and grabbed a pen and paper and placed it on a book that was sitting on the coffee table. "Okay, so let's lay out both of your options. Walter Reed's option and NIH, okay? Maybe if they are written down we can blatantly see what the right choice is."

"Wait, there are three options," Gary said.

"No, Gary, only two right?" I asked.

"You're forgetting that everyone is saying 'Watchful Waiting.' They can just follow my blood count and hope it doesn't get worse. Basically do nothing now."

"You really aren't considering that are you?" I asked.

"No, not at all, I want to get started on something as soon as I can," he promised. "The thought of knowing that I have cancer in my body and to do nothing is something I cannot fathom. I'm feeling perfectly fine now, so now is the time to attack those fucking Mantle cells."

"Well thank God for that!" I exclaimed. I wrote both of the options across the top of the paper. We would list the pros and cons of each. Deep down, I knew his choice, but we had to discuss it to make sure. *Leave no stone unturned*, I thought. I knew he would decide on the NIH. The reasons would become very apparent.

"Okay," I said, "let's put down what we know about the NIH protocol." There was a clinical trial at the NIH for newly diagnosed Mantle Cell patients. It was a chemotherapy regime, called EPOCH-R.B

I started the list:

- NIH-EPOCH-R with Bortezomib (a proteasome inhibitor)

- Chemo cycle- five days of infusion every three weeks

- Blood work twice a week until the white blood cell count comes back up. This would mean driving up to NIH (30 miles away).

- PICC (Peripherally inserted central catheter) line the day of procedure, to stay in for the five days of chemo infusion.

- Backpack of chemo therapeutic agents to take home. Come back daily to change out chemo bag, during those five days.

- Mega doses of Prednisone, as a large dose will kill the cells.

- Neupogen shots to increase and stimulate the production of white cells after chemo ends and when the white cells are at the lowest.

- Weakened immune system when white cells at lowest. Very susceptible to infections during this time.

- Platelets would be low during that time and at risk for bleeding.

- No overnights if all goes well.

- Will lose hair.

- Can continue to work if all goes well.

"What am I leaving out Gary?" I asked.

"Well, there is a lot more, but that is it basically. It's amazing how they came up with that name, EPOCH-RB as it is a combination of old and new names and generic and brand names. And then the new chemotherapy agent, Bortizamib, they didn't even have proteasomes when I was in medical school. It wasn't until 1995! Anyhow, I probably will feel like crap and I may get peripheral neuropathies. Do you know what that is?" he asked. "It's a nerve issue and I would probably experience a loss of sensation in my extremities. I'm sure there is a lot more than that, but I guess I won't know until I go through a cycle or two."

"Now let's write down the information for what Walter Reed is suggesting," I said.

Walter Reed - Autologous stem cell transplant.

- Great team of doctors.

- In hospital for a long time as immune system would be very compromised, wiped out.

- Chemo to suppress the white cells hoping that the mantle cells are most.

- Give Neupogen (Filgrastim) to stimulate production of own white cells and stem cells.

- Then Apheresis which harvests stem cells, it takes cells out and then puts back the ones that aren't stem cells. Then they preserve the stem cells.

- Then they completely wipe out the bone marrow, with chemical agents or radiation.

- Immune system has been eliminated, high risk for infections and bleeding.

- Three weeks to 6 months in the hospital.

Gary stopped me from writing and said, "Jane, I think I know what I have to do, it's pretty obvious, isn't it?"

I knew where he was going with this but I needed to hear him say it.

"What?" I implored. "What do you think the best option is?"

"It's obviously the NIH." I can't go with the Autologous Stem Cell Transplant! I can't be in the hospital all of that time! How would we survive doing that? I have to work, I have to make an income... we live in the freaking DC area and we need to make payments on this house! You know, it could even kill me, having that done. That is such a HUGE risk for me right off of the bat. I really think that there is only one choice for me right now, do you agree Jane?"

"Totally, but I wanted you to be able to see it on paper and see what the best option for you would be. Maybe we can think about the Autologous Stem Cell Transplant in the future, put it in our back pocket and save it for when you really might need it, though I hope you never will," I said.

"Well that's it, we have decided," he said. "But why don't I feel any better about this? How can I, as both choices are really the pits?"

I grabbed his hand and gave it the double squeeze; our 'I love you' sign. I didn't need to say any more, there were no more words except to let him know that I would support whatever decision he/we decided on.

While still holding my hand, he turned to me and said, "Let's get this going soon! I want this disgusting ugly cancer to get out of my system, and the sooner the better. I'll call both NIH and Walter Reed tomorrow and let them know 'our' decision. Cancer is not going to define me. I may have cancer but cancer doesn't have me. Is that a quote from a movie, or did I come up with that on my own?"

He reached for me and held me and rested his chin on the top of my head and said, "I don't want to let you go Jane; I love our closeness and our reaching these tough decisions together. Holding you just makes everything alright.

God, I'm lucky to have you in my life!"

I'm glad he couldn't see me, but I really didn't care if he did… the tears just freely flowed.

CHAPTER 26

Let it Snow

"Elizabeth, please, please, please don't leave today, the weather is supposed to be terrible! We are expecting a major snow storm and I don't want you on the road," I pleaded into the phone.

"Mom, I'm fine, we are fine!" declared Elizabeth. "I promise to take it slow, okay? You know those forecasters; they never get it right about the weather. Plus I plan on leaving soon before any of this is supposed to begin. I'm sure I will miss it all. If I wait until tomorrow it might be really bad and then who knows when I will get there!"

"I just don't need one more thing to worry about, you know?" I exclaimed. "Dealing with your Dad and his chemo and now with Christmas a week away, oh I don't know. I'm just worried! Sorry to be such a nervous Nellie."

Preparing for the holidays had been a challenge as we had been dealing with so much; chemo days and then the after effects of it. Meanwhile we were both working and trying to get ready for family arriving at the house, which meant decorating, baking and cleaning. I wasn't in the mood, not at all, but I knew that I needed to get in that spirit, Gary needed it, he needed laughter and fun! I also knew that once Elizabeth and the kids arrived, I would be fine. They, especially Mattie and JT, needed and deserved a happy Christmas as their Daddy was in Iraq with the National Guard.

"Okay," I acquiesced, "but please keep me posted of your progress!"

It was December 18th, 2009 and the only thing on the television and radio was the news of the 'possible' big snow storm that was supposed to hit the east coast. It was rumored to start late in the evening, so we were probably just fine, no worries, Elizabeth would make it in plenty of time before things got bad.

I glanced out the window as I hung up the phone. Good, I said to myself, nothing yet, but then it was only 2:00. Elizabeth was already on her way, as she was in the process of picking up JT from school. After that, they would head out right from there, stop in Yanceyville, North Carolina to drop off one of her biological father's dogs she had been watching and then head up the back roads through Virginia.

I opened up the back door and looked out. I could smell it, the smell of cold weather, and the smell the atmosphere gets just before the snow begins to fall. I knew that smell well as I grew up in the mid-west, most of the time in Cuyahoga Falls, Ohio. Heck I was born during a blizzard in Sheboygan, Wisconsin! We would get major snows in Ohio, lake effect snow, from Lake Erie. I knew about weather in that area and how it could turn on a dime. I shuddered, reminiscing and closed the door.

The day passed slowly and I kept running to the window. Drat! The snow showers had begun and it was only 4:30. It was mild, just little flakes slowly meandering down through the cloud filled skies. Darkness was beginning to claim its hold on the last remnants of daylight.

I stared at the phone, willing it to ring and startled myself when it rang! "Mom, we just left Dad's and are heading up and we are near the Virginia border. If all goes well we should be in by 8:30."

"What's the weather like?" I asked, trying to show a sense of calmness in my voice.

"Just light snow Mom, don't worry." Elizabeth was just trying to protect me as later I found out that the ground there was already covered and the roads were starting to get slick, but she decided not to worry me.

"Well, I do worry," I said, "as I know you are going up through the mountains and who knows what the weather will be like. Please keep me posted, okay? You have precious cargo on board and I want you to be very, very careful. You have to promise me! No texting while driving, okay?"

Elizabeth laughed and said, "I know that Mom, and I promise you! I will have JT text you to let you know how things are going, okay?"

We got off the phone and I plopped into the sofa. Fergus and Mack saw an opportunity and both made a beeline for the couch and curled up on either side of me. I let my thoughts drift over the past several weeks. It would be hard for Elizabeth and the kids seeing Gary now, as he had just lost all of his hair from the effects of the chemo.

We were out to dinner on December 8th at our favorite little Italian restaurant, Villa Bella. "Jane, I think I am beginning to lose my hair! I noticed some hairs in my mouth today from my beard" he said. "Several, as a matter of fact."

I reached over and ran my fingers through his beard and pulled back as if I had been shocked. "Whoa", I said, "isn't it a bit early for this?"

"Unfortunately it isn't," he said while grabbing for a big piece of bruschetta, "this is about the right time for it to be happening I think."

"Well, my oh my." I exclaimed putting my hand to my heart, pretending I was a southern belle. "What are we evah to do? Shall we check when we get home? Do you want to shave it tonight or what?"

"Let's just see," he murmured. "Maybe it is just a few hairs and we can hold off. I don't think so though, it seems like there are more than a few. It's a good thing I have that hair appointment with Shahnaz tomorrow, who knows she may be shaving my head!"

We arrived back at home around 30 minutes later and Gary immediately made a beeline for our bathroom. "What do you think I should use to see if there are more hairs ready to come out?" he asked.

"You know, I just don't know. We could comb it and see what happens or some sort of tape I guess, but please, not duct tape! I know you use it for everything, but that is just a bit too harsh!" I chided.

"I know, don't worry, duct tape sounds painful!" Gary exclaimed, "How about us using those sticky lint papers, you know, the ones we use on our clothes to get all of the dog hair off of them?"

He placed one sheet on the side of his face, covering his beard and then gently pulled the paper back. The paper was covered with hair! We both looked at the paper and then looked at each other. We didn't know if we should laugh or cry! Gary broke the ice and said, "Well that's that, I guess the mustache and beard are going tonight and then Shahnaz can shave my head tomorrow! Hey, why don't you get the camera and we will start taking pictures of the progress."

I knew he was trying so hard to keep the conversation light. We both knew this day was coming and come it did, with a vengeance. We made the most of it and I took silly pictures of the events of the evening capturing a bizarre half-shaved beard and then just a pencil thin mustache. We laughed so hard at the sight of it that tears were coming down our cheeks.

The next day Gary sat in the chair at Dolce Vita, our salon in McLean, VA. Shahnaz said, "Gary, are you sure? You really really want me to shave it all off?"

"Shahnaz, I have no choice in this, it is coming out rapidly and it is very spotty on the top of my head, so it will just look odd if I try to keep it, so off it comes!" Gary exclaimed.

Shahnaz kept up with our antics and gave him a shave to remember. At one point I believe we had a form of a Mohawk going on. I again grabbed the camera and captured the moments. "Lighthearted," I thought, "Just what we need."

I was aroused from my thoughts by the ringing of the phone. "Hey there, I'm on my way home!" Gary said cheerfully. "Is Elizabeth on her way?"

"Wow, what time is it?" I asked. "Oh, my gosh, is it really 6:30? I got off the phone with Elizabeth about 4:30 and she was on her way from Mike's house and I sat down on the couch to get my mind off of the weather and I guess I dozed off! I hope she is okay on the roads. What's it like out there?"

"No doubts that you needed a rest, you have been running around like crazy, but that is what you always do at this time of the year. You want to make it perfect for the kids, don't you? The roads don't look bad at all Jane, stop worrying!"

"I want to make it perfect for you too, you know," I stated. "The holidays have always been such a magical time for me, for us, and I want to keep that up, even though we are going through hell right now."

"I do appreciate it, you don't how much I do, but it means a lot to me Jane," Gary said, with a catch in his voice.

He had been pretty emotional lately, but actually I didn't think that was so bad. He wasn't crying all the time, just more sensitive and also seemed to be more intuitive to others' feelings to include his own.

"Well, get on the road soon and come home and worry with me about Elizabeth on the road," I said. "I hate that she is driving in this!"

"I'll see you in about 45 minutes. Can I stop and bring something home?" he asked.

"No, I have some chicken soup in the crock pot, perfect on a night like tonight!" I exclaimed.

I hung up with Gary and immediately called Elizabeth. No answer…what the heck?

The phone rang 30 seconds later. "Sorry Mom, I couldn't get to the phone when you called," said Elizabeth. "Traffic is crawling and I am only up to the Lynchburg area. It's snowing but the road is mostly visible, so stop worrying, because I know that you are! I promise to keep you posted."

We said our good-byes and I hung up the phone. Ha, no worrying… right! Traffic crawling and she had only traveled a very short distance in two hours. Come on Jane, you can do this. I busied myself in the kitchen. I fed the dogs and then opened the back door to let them out. The ground was covered with a blanket of fresh fallen snow. I stood on the deck and watched Fergus, the Border Collie, delight in the weather. Big flakes were cascading down and landing everywhere, and some landed on the top of Fergus' nose. He leapt in the air trying to bite at them. I laughed at the site. There were only a couple of inches of snow on the ground and it was a beautiful site.

There was such a silence in the air, a crisp silence. I loved that sound, or lack thereof. The quietness of the snow as it falls from the heavens, such a very peaceful sound and feeling. I then realized that I had been shivering and that my hair was just covered in the white stuff and made my way back in the house with the two dogs following right behind, hoping for dog treats when they got inside.

I was relieved when I heard the garage door go up knowing that Gary was home. It took longer than the 45 minutes he thought it would take, closer to an hour. The weather was getting worse and the roads were beginning to get covered.

We settled in for a lovely winter meal, just the two of us, both of us worrying about Elizabeth but not wanting to worry each other, so small talk was the flavor of the evening. It was a Friday night so Gary could relax, knowing that he did not have to go into work the next day.

"Gary, I'm going to go out and shovel and don't tell me I can't," I said. "I don't want you to do it with your immune system so compromised from all of the chemo. Your job is to listen out for the phone for Elizabeth, got it??"

"I hate to have you do it, especially as you have such a weak back, but you are right, I shouldn't be shoveling, thanks. Hey maybe it will take your mind off of Elizabeth and the grandkids," he said.

There were about 4 inches on the ground by the time I got out there at 8:00 so it really wasn't too difficult to do. Within 45 minutes I had completed my task and headed in the house. Waiting for me was a mug of hot chocolate that Gary had just made.

"You've done all the hard work, here's something to warm those toes, plus there's an extra kick of a bit of alcohol in it!" he exclaimed. "I heard from Liz, she is stuck about 40 miles out of Charlottesville and has been for over an hour. They aren't moving and the weather is getting bad."

"Oh damn," I said taking the mug. "What is she going to do? Oh and by the way, thank you, this is delicious!"

"She heard on the radio that there is a truck stuck up the road a short distance away. Hopefully it will get cleared and she can head out."

Two hours later Elizabeth called and stated that the road she was on was being closed and they were all told to turn back. "Mom, what are we going to do? I have two kids with me, a dog and a snake!"

I sensed the panic in her voice and tried to remain calm.

Gary saw from the look on my face that I was worried and asked if he could talk to Elizabeth. I gladly handed the phone over to him.

"Hey Liz, no worries, I think your best bet is to drive back to Lynchburg less than 30 miles away. Turn around and start heading that way and I will call a hotel and get reservations made for all of you. Are you guys okay?" he calmly asked.

"We are warm and snug, but damn, the roads are just crappy. I can hardly see where to go! Don't tell Mom, as you know how uptight she gets about bad weather!" Elizabeth pleaded.

"It's okay Liz, we've got you covered. Just take it slow and relax. Have JT help guide you on the roads all right? Call me if you need to talk," he said.

We got off the phone and I began to pace with worry. "Jane, that isn't helping her," Gary said. "Let's look for a hotel for Liz and the kids in Lynchburg. I am sure we will be able to find something, let's just hope they take pets!"

"Liz," Gary said, "as luck would have it, the first place we tried had 2 rooms left and they will take pets, so I booked the room, they are holding it for you… How far away from Lynchburg are you now?"

"Thanks, Fwah! Oh what a relief! Well I have only gone about 3 miles since we last talked, traffic is painfully slow and the weather is horrendous!" she moaned.

An hour later, midnight, she arrived at the hotel safe and sound. We were so eager to get that call hearing the words that they were safe. I knew she had to be exhausted from such a tense and worrisome drive. "We are going to try to head up tomorrow," she said.

"Liz, the weather is still getting worse, I don't think you will be going anywhere as the plows aren't going to be able to clear all of this that quickly," Gary told her. "Just relax and give us a call in the morning and let us know how everything is. We will take it from there."

I looked at Gary after we hung up the phone. He reached his arms out to me for a major hug. "I can't take all of this stress," I said. "I am so relieved that she and the kids are safe in the hotel room, I feel like I can finally take a deep breath! I was so worried that her car would go off the road!" It felt fantastic to feel Gary's strong arms around me, letting me know that the worst had passed and we now could relax and maybe even get some much needed sleep.

We woke up the next morning to a winter wonderland with snow still continuing to fall. I made several trips outside to try to keep the drive and sidewalks shoveled. It was a huge amount of work, but I was determined not to have Gary do any of it. The chemo made him weak and his immune system wasn't functioning well, so he had no business going out. Ian couldn't come over and help us as he couldn't get out of his neighborhood so it was up to me to get it done.

Liz made the determination to stay in Lynchburg another night, as the roads were just covered all around her and snow plows were struggling to keep up with it. We went online and found an open restaurant nearby where she was staying. It was a place that she and the kids were able to walk to and have some decent meals. Her hopes for traveling on Sunday paid off, and though the roads were still terrible, they arrived safe and sound on Sunday evening. Twenty inches of snow fell in that snow storm, the most ever in the Washington, DC area for a December. My back felt every bit of it from all of the shoveling! Little did we know but that was just one of several storms we were to receive that season, but that was the only one that Liz had to deal with. I am sure the events of that trip will be forever etched in her brain.

Gary worried how the grandchildren would react to his

different look. He had a plan. After everyone was settled in the house and many stories were told about the horrendous weather, Gary handed Mattie and JT an eyebrow pencil and said, "I know that my bald head looks pretty darn weird to you so why don't you both just have some fun. Draw on my head any way you want to!"

The art work was pretty pathetic, with a face drawn on the back of his head and fake curls everywhere. Pictures were taken of smiling grandchildren and grandfather. It surely changed the demeanor in the room and within minutes everyone was laughing and joking; Fwah wasn't scary, he was fun!

It was a Christmas to remember in so many ways but in other ways, one that we were willing to soon forget. I knew I had made the right decision to have the house filled with family as it surely was the world's greatest distracter. But I made sure to keep a close eye on Gary, I didn't want him to become overly tired or get exposed to someone's sniffles. It was a balance that I knew I needed to keep in check… he was my number one concern.

CHAPTER 27

Blog posts and emails

Coping

Dealing with the diagnosis of Mantle Cell Lymphoma.

Tuesday, October 27, 2009

<u>Well meaning 'friends':</u>

Tell me why it is when someone hears your story about cancer that they feel they must share every terrible thing that they know about it and then tell me how someone they know had some form of cancer and suffered terribly and died??? Why do they think I want to hear this? Don't they know that I am just coming to grips with it myself and hearing the 'worst case scenario' is not being helpful? I just nod my head and listen, but inside I am going I just can't stand to hear you talk!

Chemo begins this coming Monday, a Clinical Trial up at the NIH Cancer Institute in Bethesda, MD.

We are on an emotional roller coaster and I have to stop crying and start being supportive and strong. When will that happen?

Monday, November 2, 2009

<u>Chemo begins</u>

Am I relieved or am I scared out of my mind? Today starts the first round of chemo for Gary and I don't know how to feel. Right now I am feeling a quite numb about it all.

I hardly slept last night thinking about it and finally got up at 3:45 and got in the shower. Why stay in bed when my mind just won't shut off?

We have had a great weekend and a great distraction. Our dear friends from Massachusetts came to visit us. It has been a huge distraction and for that I am grateful. We had a Halloween party and friends came over to include our son, his wife and baby. It was excellent! Gary's friend helped him in the basement, getting it framed so we can finally get walls up. That is huge.

We will leave for the hospital in about an hour.

November 21, 2009

The Mega Chemo has begun:

Gary had his first round of Bortezomib and completed that a week ago. Yesterday was the mega day for chemo. He was at NIH all day; got a lovely cocktail of meds in his IV to include taking some home so it would be infused over a 24 hour period. He has a pump and an IV bag and it goes in his arm through a PICC line. He has to go back every day and get the bag changed out. That goes on until Tuesday and then they give him a mega dose of something (can't remember the name now) and it is the one that could make him feel really crappy. So far, he is doing fine with no side effects. He was a bit nauseated on the way home from chemo yesterday, but it was probably my driving! It was rush hour and there was a lot of starting and stopping. That was it for side effects. Oh, and he is on a whopping dose of prednisone. 140 mg twice a day for 5 days! Every 3 weeks, he will get this round of stuff.... Hair should be falling out in a couple of weeks.

I hate this for him... I hate this for him... I hate this for him.

December 27, 2009

Excerpts from our Christmas Letter:

Dear Family and Friends:

Gary continues to work for the Department of Defense in Health Affairs. It is a very busy job and he works very long hours. The usual day is from 7:00-7:00.

Our world fell apart in October of this year. Gary got a call stating his routine blood count was off and he needed to have more tests done. That he did, to include CT scans, tons of blood work, PET scan, and a bone marrow biopsy. The results showed that he was in Stage 4 Mantle Cell Lymphoma. We were sure that the blood work issues were out of whack from all of the medications he is on; we had no clue that this was a new issue. Since this time he has begun a clinical trial at the National Institutes for Health (NIH) at the cancer institute. To this date he has received two rounds of a combination of medicines called EPOCH-R. It is a heavy duty mixture. Here are the websites with the information of all of the chemo meds that Gary is on:

http://www.chemocare.com/bio/list_by_acronym. asp?acronym=EPOCH%2BR
http://www.chemocare.com/bio/bortezomib.asp
http://www.chemocare.com/bio/neupogen.asp

Three weeks ago, his hair began falling out. He has taken

it in stride and is making the most (or the least) of it, to include finding outrageous hats to wear! His sense of humor

is there as is his positive attitude! I am not saying that we haven't had a tough time with

the diagnosis, as we really did and spent many a day crying over it. We decided to just

take a day at a time and are now dealing and coping with it in a much more positive

way.

On that note I will end this letter on a more positive note! Keep Gary in your thoughts

and prayers, and help keep James safe in Iraq. May your 2010 be everything you

are hoping for and more!

Sunday, January 17, 2010

<u>Mouth sores:</u>

Once the crampy abdomen started resolving, the mouth sores came with a vengeance. It was so terrible he could hardly open his mouth. It was another week of a liquid diet, smoothies and popsicles and oragel to help numb the mouth.

The only good thing to come out of it was that on Monday after his routine blood work, we found out that he had reached his nadir. He was at the lowest for his white blood cell count, below 500 (normal between 4-10,000). This meant that the chemo was working... but also meant that his immune system was hanging on by a thread. He wanted to continue to work and I was angry about it. He could pick up any bug imaginable! He promised me he would go to work and not attend meetings unless he could call in to the meeting. By Thursday his blood count had gone up to a normal range and I could stop giving him the neupogen shots. He had been having them for 8 days straight, but they did their work and elevated the white count.

On Thursday he called and said he ate a Big Mac for lunch! I knew he was 'on the mend'!! This weekend has been a good weekend, and he has felt pretty good, even doing projects around the house.

Next Friday begins a new round of chemo for him, round 4 of six.

We will enjoy these great days this week and hope that this next round won't make him too miserable and the worst is behind him.

Monday, March 8, 2010

<u>Update on life:</u>

It has been close to two months since I have added anything to my blog. It isn't that there isn't anything going on; it is just that I have had a difficult time finding a few moments to write.

As I write this, Gary is receiving his last round (#6) of chemo. The final dose being delivered tomorrow. What happens after that is re-staging. That will begin on the 24th of this month and then subsequent days after. He will have a CT scan, PET scan, bone marrow biopsy, colonoscopy and lots of blood work.

How is he doing??? Unfortunately the Bortezomib had

to be stopped for the 5th and 6th round, due to peripheral neuropathy and now the Vincrisitine was stopped for the last round, the 6th one. His legs are swollen, especially the right lower leg and foot and the pain and tingling are present. We are hoping that it will improve over time, but there is no guarantee of that. He is doing well, other than that and seems to be tolerating everything else quite well.

A few weeks ago, we visited with Gary's neurologist to discuss his neuropathies and his Parkinson's. After a very thorough appointment (3 hours) it was great to hear that though his Parkinson's is progressing, it is minimal. That is such a relief. Unfortunately the peripheral neuropathies are real and with an extensive exam proved very much to be so. We are hoping it will eventually improve once the chemo ends.

We are adjusting... life is far from normal. It's as if the elephant has moved into our house and is hiding behind a very sheer curtain. It is there, but we aren't discussing it. How much can one discuss it without breaking down all the time?
I think once his hair returns and the IV's are out that we can move on. Right now it is so ever present.

We don't talk as much as we have in the past. It is stressful for Gary as it is for me. I guess it is hard to look to the future until we hear what the results of the re-staging are. We are disappointed that some of the chemo meds had to be taken away and worry about what that means for the future.

Last month, on the 19th of February, my sister-in-law, BL, lost her fight with cancer. She hung on for 21 months from diagnosis, which was way above what was expected. She was told about 7 months. I went to the funeral in Kentucky and Gary stayed home. I am sure it is very difficult for him to hear about all of this. It was horrendous for me, but I needed to be there for my brother. He is in my thoughts all of the time.

Our friends are such a support to us, especially our Boston friends, Andy and Susie and our friends here, Diane and Bill. Andy has come down here for several of Gary's chemos and Susie has been such a huge support for me. Andy is helping Gary with finishing our basement. It has been a great distraction for both of them. Andy is Gary's best friend and his support through all of this has been such an important part of the process. Bill has come over several times also to help in the basement and having the continued friendship with both of them has made all of the difference.

Wednesday, March 10, 2010

<u>Celebration:</u>

Gary's last round of chemo was yesterday. The PICC line is out and now it is dealing with the chemo side effects and then re-staging in 2 weeks. The nurses came into his room as the last drip of Cytoxan was leaving the bag and sang 'For he's a jolly good fellow' and gave him a cake. How sweet is that?

We went to our son and his wife's house after to celebrate with a pizza and champagne (sparkling juice for Gary). It was great to be with family on such a momentous day.

Wednesday, March 24, 2010

Accident with Mercedes:

We were on our way to NIH for many tests for Gary's re-staging. I was in my car and a few miles in front of Gary who was in a Mercedes SLK 280, a very small black car, but very cute!

Gary was on 495 North, inner loop, heading towards Bethesda. He had just passed I66 (entrance ramp from I66 to 495 is on the left) and Gary was in the far right lane. He observed an 18 wheeler entering 495 from I66 and watched as it crossed 3 lanes of traffic and was heading towards him. Gary was honking his horn and flashing his lights, to no avail, as the trucker had no idea that he was there.

The truck continued on over into Gary's lane and Gary tried to speed up to get by him, but no such luck. The front right wheel of the 18 wheeler hooked onto the driver's side of Gary's car. Literally, they were hooked together traveling down the road. Finally the trucker realized what was going on and stopped. I'm sure the noise must have been deafening!

The whole driver's side of Gary's car was dented and torn apart, but Gary walked away without a scratch! Well he didn't walk away too quickly as he was pinned in between the truck and the Jersey wall. The EMS suggested he try to take the convertible top down and have him climb out that way. It worked!

Traffic was backed up for several miles because of the accident, and even made the news.

Gary called me right after it happened and said 'Jane, I've been in an accident but I am okay, a truck hit me'. At that point I didn't know if the car was drivable so I drove back thinking I might be able to help him and drive him back to

NIH. As I drove past the scene, which is when I found out that it was an 18 wheeler... I couldn't believe it!

Now what is even more amazing, the car was drivable and he made it to NIH in plenty of time for his appointment. After the tests he drove to the Mercedes dealer and turned the car in and got a loaner. We were afraid the car was totaled, but luckily it was only $5000 worth of damage and is being repaired now.

Here I am being very analytical about this, but when I think about what could have happened I begin to cry. What an amazingly lucky man he is!

April 6, 2010 Email:

Dear friends and family,

My email to you in December was telling you about Gary's cancer, Mantle Cell lymphoma. He has been receiving treatment at the NIH and is in a clinical trial. He completed the series of 7 chemo treatments, suffered from miserable side effects (never enough to lose a day of work!) and lost all of his hair. Two weeks ago it was time for his re-staging. He was at stage 4 prior to the chemo. I am happy to report to you that he is in REMISSION!!!! No trace of mantle cell in every test they gave him (CT scan, PET scan, blood work, bone marrow biopsy and colonoscopy). We are so delighted with the news and just feel like celebrating.
The doctors at NIH don't want to see him until the end of June, so the chemo has stopped for a while (hopefully for a LONG time!).